THE LONG ROUTES

THE LONG ROUTES

Mountaineering Rock Climbs in Snowdonia and the Lake District

ROBIN ASHCROFT

MAINSTREAM
PUBLISHING
EDINBURGH AND LONDON

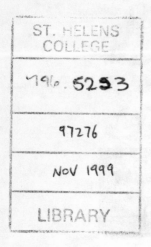
First published in Great Britain in 1999 by
MAINSTREAM PUBLISHING COMPANY (EDINBURGH) LTD
7 Albany Street
Edinburgh   EH1 3UG

ISBN 1 85158 910 4

A CIP catalogue record for this book is available from the British Library

Typeset in Stone and Garamond
Printed and bound in Great Britain by Butler & Tanner Ltd

Dedicated to the memory of Captain David Wolfe
The King's Own Royal Border Regiment
1961–1987

CONTENTS

Part Two: Snowdonia

ACKNOWLEDGEMENTS

Anyone who writes about the mountains and cliffs of Snowdonia or the Lake District owes a debt of gratitude to the endeavours of the editors and writers of the established guides published by the Climbers' Club and the Fell and Rock-Climbing Club; they are the 'bedrock' of climbing in these areas. It is hoped that any interest generated by this book will lead to an increased appreciation of these marvellous works.

I would like to acknowledge that the inspiration to seek out these types of route was first provided by Ken Wilson's *Classic Rock* and also by Steve Ashton's *100 Classic Climbs* series.

The preparation of this guidebook would have been impossible without the unstinting support – sometimes without realising it, and over a number of years – of many people. I'd like to thank them all: Dave Aizlewood, Clive Allen, Audrey Ashcroft, Bryan Ashcroft, Jeremy Ashcroft, Ross Ashe-Creggan, Ian Atkins, Tim Barret, Hugh Harris, Ed Kenyon, John Kitchiner, David Ogle, Andrew Sydenham, Vicky Tebbs and Steve Udberg.

Special mention must go to Tony Shewell's input on the photography and to his skill at holding a falling leader. Finally, special thanks to Deborah Scott-Ashcroft and Olivia Scott-Ashcroft for being so understanding about my weekends away and the time I spent in front of the computer.

Robin Ashcroft
Cartmel
April 1999

PREFACE

Sometime between the 27 and 30 June 1886, William Parry Haskett-Smith was coming to the end of his holiday at Wasdale Head. Suffering from a headache he took to the fells to try to walk it off. This he did successfully; and in an improved frame of mind turned his attention to – and then climbed, for the first time and by himself – Napes Needle.

Educated at Eton and Oxford – where he indulged in 'night climbing on the spires' – he was a well-regarded member of the fraternity of those Victorian gentleman mountaineers who regularly based themselves at Wasdale Head. By the time he first climbed Napes Needle he had been to the Alps, the Rockies, the Andes and Norway. He had also put up a number of new routes in the British mountains including Needle Ridge, on Napes on Great Gable.

Needle Ridge is, of course, named after Napes Needle – a free-standing pillar of rock some forty-odd feet in height – at the base of the ridge. Needle Ridge was first climbed in 1884. The motivation being that it provided a logical route up the rock of Napes and on to the summit of Great Gable.

Two years later, Haskett-Smith returned to the Needle, and his ensuing, successful, first ascent is generally regarded – although one doubts if this was foremost in his mind at the time – as being a watershed. It is seen as the start of rock-climbing as a separate sport that is within the boundaries of mountaineering but at the same time as a distinct entity. By climbing Napes Needle, the focus was shifted from climbing a piece of rock in order to reach a mountain's summit to climbing a piece of rock as a pursuit in its own right.

The purpose of recounting this story is to try to provide a useful definition for the term 'mountaineering rock-climb' in the context of this book. It is a climb that has its own inherent worth but it is

13

also part of the mountain's whole structure and a route to the summit. As a rule of thumb, Needle Ridge is very definitely a mountaineering route, while Napes Needle – despite its real challenge and the fun it provides – isn't.

It's also an opportunity to reflect on the skill and determination of the 'Father of rock-climbing' – as anyone who has climbed the Needle will acknowledge – who not only undertook that first horrendous mantleshelf on the Needle but also climbed back down again. All without the benefit of a companion's moral support or a rope, and in nailed boots! There must be something in an education at Eton and Oxford.

INTRODUCTION

The aim of this book is to help people seek out and climb long, adventurous climbs on the high-mountain cliffs of Snowdonia and the Lake District – ideally taking in a summit in the process. On these routes – of a grade between Difficult and Hard Severe – technical difficulty takes second place to the exhilaration at the scale of the climbing and the exposed situation of the route.

The main appeal of these climbs lies in seeking out and following the most logical way up a cliff, as well as reaching the summit. The approach to the mountain is holistic and well removed from viewing the crag as an end in itself.

Many of the routes included in this guide were first climbed when the mountain cliffs were originally explored around the turn of the century. Then, climbers had the luxury of having acres of untouched rock and the pick of the best natural features and, as a result, these routes have an elegance and simplicity all of their own.

Of course, both rock-climbing and mountaineering have moved on, and the very natural desire to finish a first ascent is strong. As a result, modern rock-climbers are often highly skilled and aggressive athletes who can complete amazing climbs. The routes outlined in this book are often dismissed as 'old-fashioned' when set against modern test pieces. This is a shame, as the routes which are covered in this guide can provide superb and demanding expeditions that call upon the full range of a mountaineer's skills. They require stamina, determination, judgement and ability, as well as the enthusiasm for space below your feet and a willingness to commit to a long route on a high-mountain cliff. Also, they will take you to places where solitude can still be found.

USING THIS GUIDE

In this book you will find both route descriptions of some of the best of the mountaineering rock-climbs in Snowdonia and the Lake District, as well as practical information on how to climb them in a safe and enjoyable way.

The sections on equipment and techniques aren't intended to be a comprehensive instructional manual on either mountaineering or rock-climbing. They will, however, focus on the specific problems and techniques involved in climbing long, multi-pitch rock-climbs in a high-mountain environment.

The route descriptions are set out by mountain area with information of the approach, the routes themselves and both descent route and associated mountain walks. They are supported by a crag diagram (to help identify the route on the cliff) and a topographical diagram (to provide a detailed visual outline of the route). It must be emphasised that you should also use either an Ordnance Survey or Harvey's Map for both planning and travelling.

Each route guide will follow the standard format.

INFORMATION BLOCK
➤ **Mountain:** On which the route will be found, along with the height of the principal summit.
➤ **Cliff:** Where the climb is.
➤ **Location:** The grid reference for the climb.
➤ **Grade:** The overall technical grade of the climb.
➤ **Height:** The total height of the climb.
➤ **Time:** How long it will take a reasonably fit and experienced party to complete the approach, the climb itself and the recommended way to take in a summit.
➤ **Parking:** The nearest point to the climb where you leave the road.
➤ **Maps:** Appropriate Ordnance Survey sheets (1:25000 and 1:50000) and Harvey's maps (1:25000 and 1:40000).

➤ **Guidebooks:** The comprehensive Fell and Rock-Climbing Club (F&RCC) or Climbers' Club (CC) guide that covers the area.
➤ **Equipment:** An indication of the most useful equipment for each climb. This list assumes that essential equipment such as helmet, specified harness, climbing ropes and a comprehensive selection of protection devices, slings and sufficient karabiners will be carried as a matter of good sense. No mention is made of appropriate mountain clothing or emergency gear.
➤ **Accommodation:** The most convenient and economic accommodation that provides open access to a bed, hot showers and a drying-room. In the main these will be Youth Hostels.

LAYOUT OF TEXT
➤ **Introduction:** A brief introduction to the climb, highlighting its attractions, difficulties and other points of interest.
➤ **Situation:** Establishing the location, appearance and typical condition of the climb.
➤ **Route:** An objective pitch-by-pitch description of the route.
➤ **Descent:** How to get off the cliff and mountain at the end of the climb by the safest and quickest way, along with some suggestions for taking in the nearest summit and a mountain walk.

GRADING
The grades used in this guidebook are the standard UK adjective grading system that ascends in progressive order: Easy, Moderate, Difficult, Hard Difficult, Very Difficult, Hard Very Difficult, Mild Severe, Severe, Hard Severe, Very Severe and Extreme. All routes listed in this book fall between Difficult and Hard Severe. This grading system is a compromise between the overall technical difficulty, the level of exposure and the objective risk of the complete climb, rather than individual pitches. On climbs of the technical standard found in this book, it isn't usual to quote the technical grade pitch by pitch. For a general comparison: the grade of Severe equates to a technical grade of 4a; a UIAA grade of IV; and a USA grade of 5.5.

CRAG DIAGRAM

A crag diagram is included to help locate the climb on the cliff and its general line of ascent, along with any scrambling sections. Climbing sections are indicated by dashes and scrambling sections by dots.

TOPO

A detailed schematic diagram, using established symbols showing the route, pitches and type of climbing.

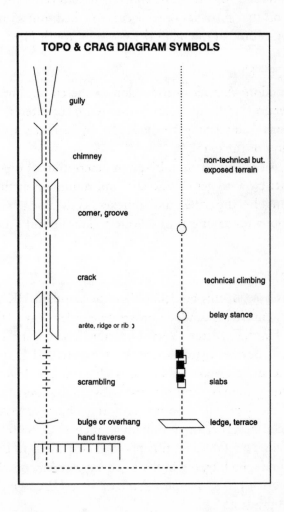

EQUIPMENT NOTES

All of the climbs in this guide are found on high-mountain cliffs, topping out just below the summit or summit ridge, often around the 900m or 3,000ft contour. While common sense dictates that you avoid setting out in bad weather, conditions can change rapidly in the mountains and you will, at some stage, find yourself high on a route with bad weather approaching. You need to be clothed and equipped to deal with it.

In addition, a multi-pitch climb places increased demands on your technical climbing gear that may not be apparent in a valley-crag environment. In particular, you will need to think about what type of footwear you use. While modern, 'sticky' climbing shoes undoubtedly make climbing easier, and probably enable you to raise your grade by several levels, they are a liability when it comes to walking and are positively dangerous on grass.

It's also important to be highly selective about what gear you take. If you pack to cover every eventuality then you won't be able to climb as well while carrying a large rucksack.

BOOTS
A significant decision and there are three options:
➤ **A modern, 'sticky', smooth-soled climbing boot or shoe:** go for the general type – that are comfortable to wear for extended periods – rather than the highly specialist, tight versions designed for climbing in the E grades. You will need to carry walking boots, however, if you have a long descent or walk off.
➤ **A general mountaineering boot:** there has been a resurgence in this type of leather boot as they can be used for walking, scrambling, rock-climbing and snow- and ice-climbing. While they aren't as convenient to climb in as sticky boots, you should be able to tackle routes up to Severe in them – providing you are used to climbing in them. The advantage is that you only

need to take one pair of boots into the hills. Plastic boots are best used for snow and ice.

➤ **An 'alpine' rock boot:** a hybrid between a general mountaineering boot and a specialist smooth-soled rock boot. These tend to be more common in the Alps but they are now available in the UK. They are of a much lighter, trimmer design than a full-blown mountaineering boot and tend to have cleated soles – often made from 'sticky' rubber – rather than smooth soles and the lacing is through eyelets rather than 'D' rings and hooks. They are meant for use below the snow line. You can readily climb rock, utilising very delicate footholds in them, and they are suitable and comfortable to walk and scramble in.

CLOTHING

A modern three-layer clothing system is best. Try to use the following combination: a base/permanent layer, a fleece top for insulation and a breathable, waterproof, outer layer jacket. This type of layered system can be readily adjusted as the conditions change. Weight constraints will probably preclude overtrousers or salopettes.

Good-quality layered socks with a wickable inner and a padded outer will go a long way in preventing foot fatigue and blisters. It is best to use the inner, thinner socks with sticky boots. A hat that can be worn under a helmet is an important item. Keeping your hands warm is vital; look for the thin, fleece gloves with grip pads. A very useful options is fingerless mitts.

In the summer you can wear some of the new synthetic, poly-cotton tops and bottoms. Several types are now available that are wickable, windproof and showerproof; ideal when the temperature is high but there is still a risk of rain – you will, however, still need to pack a fleece and fully weatherproof top. Cotton clothing – often used on valley crags and climbing walls – is unsuitable for a high-mountain environment as it has little insulation when wet.

ROPES

While you can safely climb using either a single 11mm or 2 x 9mm ropes, there is no doubt that the latter is the best option on long multi-pitch climbs. Not only do they provide increased protection – when a rope is cut after a fall over a ledge, there is a backup – it is also much easier to use them to reduce drag and, significantly, they are better at protecting a second (if rigged properly) on a traverse. They also enable you to abseil double the distance – this is an important consideration if you ever have to retreat from high up a cliff. You will also need a fully specified climbing harness to attach yourself to the rope.

CLIMBING GEAR

You will need a comprehensive range of hardware, whether you go for 'Rocks', 'Super Rocks', 'Hexcentrics' or active camming devices, such as the 'Friends' range, in a good range of sizes. A combination of the three different types across the size spectrum will probably give the most flexibility. You do need to bear in mind the weight penalty. A good option is to take one full set between two and transfer over when the lead changes.

Each person should carry three full-length slings – these have a role in rescue situations. Everyone will also need their own belaying device, the simpler the better. And, although you can abseil on a belay device, or belay with some abseil devices, it makes sense for each person to carry their own descender as it's useful to have a back-up.

Despite the trend of climbing without helmets on climbing walls and on valley crags, they play a vital role on high-mountain cliffs. They protect your head in a fall and also from the greater risk of stonefall on a mountain crag; a falling pebble reaches terminal velocity very quickly and is quite capable of splitting a human skull apart.

An equipment bandoleer is particularly useful on multi-pitch climbs as it enables protection devices to be transferred much more conveniently – thus saving time – when the leads change. If your equipment is on a bandoleer then it is much easier to reach when you are climbing with a rucksack on.

For climbing in a mountaineering situation you will also need some specific extras. A 10m length of tape (bought from a reel rather than as a pre-stitched sling) is very useful – nay essential – should you want to abseil. One of the biggest problems with

23

abseiling is being unable to pull down the rope after the descent. If you are halfway down a cliff, this can be a very serious problem. Invariably, the friction of the rope over a rock anchor is the major cause of this problem. If you are able to cut a suitable length of tape to rig the anchor then you can avoid this happening. Don't be tempted to use a sling that's already in place on an abseil anchor as the friction caused by the climbing rope being pulled through previously will have weakened the old sling.

You should also carry sufficient gear to rig a self-rescue. On a high-mountain cliff it is essential to be self-sufficient. If you take a fall or become tired, it isn't always possible to be simply lowered to safe ground. A pair of prussik loops – tailored to the user's size – and a karabiner pulley could be a life-saver.

RUCKSACK
While the 50-litre rucksack is usually the most adaptable sack for all mountaineering purposes, and is readily usable on the type of climbs described here, there is no doubt that a 30- or 40-litre sack is more convenient. While most come with a plethora of straps, you can trim these down, for instance: on rock there is obviously no need for the ice-tool and crampon attachments. The cinch straps on the side are, however, essential for reducing volume and stabilising the sack once you've put all your gear in.

EMERGENCY GEAR
A map (1:25000), compass and guidebook should always be carried and are essential in an emergency situation. You should also know how to navigate accurately as the margin for error is small on top of a high crag and when you are in cloud. For this reason, a GPS, given its in-built margin for error, is no substitute for a map and compass.

If you get into trouble then a whistle is the traditional – and highly effective – method of communicating. It's no use, however, if you can't reach it, therefore you should tie one to your bandoleer. Another emergency signalling device which is highly effective is a strobe-light beacon which emits a flashing light over a large distance. There are a number developed by the yachting fraternity. They are lightweight, economical and work well.

Remember that they should never be stored with batteries in. A good headtorch is essential, particularly when dusk is advancing and you are still climbing. Finally, a first-aid kit should be carried within the party.

There's a mountaineering adage that says 'if you carry bivvy gear then you will need to use it'. The problem is, of course, the weight of the bivvy and the degree to which it slows you down. You will, however, need something if you are benighted – it happens – or have to sit out a storm or other emergency.

A good and lightweight compromise is to take some high-energy emergency rations (Kendal mint cake); a bivvy bag (either Goretex or poly) and a small foam mat. While a hot drink is always welcome in emergency situations, a stove is definitely too much of a weight penalty on a climb.

FOOD AND DRINK

You will need to take liquids and nourishment with you, as lack of energy and dehydration becomes a major issue when you are on a climb for more than half an hour. Little and often is the best approach, so carry small packets of food in your pockets. Liquids must be close to hand if you want to avoid the debilitating and dangerous effects of dehydration. Some duct tape, climbing tape and a small 'gear-only karabiner' can be used to rig your water bottle to hang from your bandoleer or harness. Another option is a small (roughly 0.5 litres), polythene fluid sack that can be kept in a jacket pocket.

TECHNIQUE NOTES

It isn't intended that this section of the book should attempt to compete with the wide range of instructional climbing manuals that are currently available. Indeed, you are strongly recommended to read the BMC-endorsed, and quite excellent, *Handbook of Climbing* by Alan Fyffe and Iain Peters. Nevertheless, there are areas that are specific to multi-pitch climbs on high-mountain cliffs, that aren't necessarily apparent to someone who has come into climbing via a climbing wall or on valley crags.

The first thing to point out is that the grade that you currently climb to on a climbing wall or even a valley crag won't automatically be the grade that you are comfortable climbing on a 100m-plus cliff. A combination of a strenuous approach, wind, cold and an unexpected sense of exposure will all have a sobering effect.

Loose rock also becomes an issue, so you need to be constantly aware of it and rely on your own judgement about where to place your protection – a major consideration for those who are used to bolt-protected situations. Many of these climbs attract fewer climbers than those on valley crags, so you won't always be able to rely on polish marks and will have to trust your own route-finding skills.

Additionally, leading a route over several pitches – when your life will be dependent upon your own ability – will sap your nervous energy. Nobody has a bottomless pit of this – although experience and time on rock tends to increase your reserves – so you will have to manage and conserve it. Swapping the lead, pitch on pitch, is the usual solution.

Finally, the type of strength and skills built up on a climbing wall or valley crag are only part of the requirements needed in mountaineering. Time spent mountain walking, when navigation, stamina and hill experience are developed, is time well spent.

There are still some techniques to be aware of when climbing multi-pitch routes, even assuming that you have gained experience on single-pitch routes and have mastered the established climbing, belaying, protection and rope-management techniques.

BELAYING

Direct, semi-direct and indirect belays can all be employed effectively on a multi-pitch route. You do, of course, always have to take into account the reliability of the belay anchor – particularly for a direct belay – as unstable rock is more of an issue on a high-mountain cliff.

Either a belay device or an Italian hitch can be used. And it's certainly worth being familiar with the latter, as it is essential if you drop your main belay hardware.

The main issue on a belay stance on a multi-pitch route is the rigging of the anchor: it must be able to take an upward pull as well as a downward pull. This is absolutely essential but is often ignored. If this isn't done then a lead climber who takes only a relatively small fall is quite capable of lifting their no. 2 off their feet. And if the belay isn't rigged for an upward pull then the belayer will find themselves some feet up in the air before the belay tightens – with potentially fatal consequences.

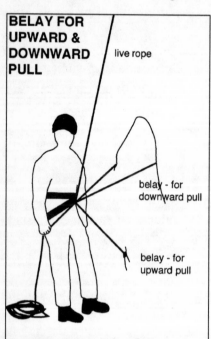

BELAY FOR UPWARD & DOWNWARD PULL

live rope

belay - for downward pull

belay - for upward pull

ABSEILING

You should be familiar with and have practised several abseiling methods, including the use of a figure of eight, the semi-classic and even the classic. The latter isn't recommended for use as a matter of course – it ruins Goretex – but is useful if you drop gear.

You also need to know how to select and rig an

abseil anchor properly. The importance of this cannot be stressed too much as it is always impossible to provide a back-up belay for the final person down. A 10m length of unstitched tape off which you can cut the required length – the single most important use for a Swiss Army penknife – should always be in the party's equipment.

The reasons for this are worth explaining: firstly, you can rig a much safer anchor if you have some flexibility in adjusting the angle of the pull. Secondly, if a rope goes directly around a wide anchor – such as a rock pillar – then the drag that can build up when you try to pull it down behind you can be considerable. This is a major contributing factor in a rope jamming. And a jammed rope, halfway down a major cliff is a very serious problem to face. Finally, it saves you a lot of money if you don't have to use, and lose, expensive stitched tapes.

Using 2 x 9mm ropes will obviously enable you to descend double the distance compared to using a single 11mm rope. For this reason alone, it makes the double-rope system a much better option on multi-pitch routes.

A double fisherman's knot, with a reef knot tied in between is the established way of tying two ropes together. The reef knot prevents the fisherman's knot from tightening to such a degree that it can't be untied.

When pulling the rope down, you must always ensure that the ropes aren't twisted around each other and that you pull down on the rope on the side of which the knot lies clear of the anchor so that the knot doesn't jam behind the sling.

You aren't always able to confirm that the rope has bottomed. And the risk of falling off the end of a rope is always there for the first person down. To stop them falling off, tie the two bottom ends together with a thumb knot and rig a prussik loop between the rope and the harness.

If the prussik knot is kept in hand and loose, it will slide down the rope. In the event that you run out of rope you will have the basis of a system for hanging there safely and then climbing back up a rope.

Finally, abseiling is possibly the riskiest technique you can employ in the mountains. At some stage, someone – the last man down – will have only one point of contact with the cliff: the abseil anchor, and will have no belay back-up. Therefore it makes sense to give the Hollywood antics a miss and always abseil in a controlled, smooth manner. That way the minimum strain is placed on the anchor. A lot of fine mountaineers have died while undertaking a 'simple' abseil. It is, however, a life-saving technique and it makes sense to learn how to abseil properly.

SELF-RESCUE

If you or your partner have become exhausted; had a fall; ended up hanging free, away from the rock face; or become unconscious, it isn't always possible to be lowered back to the ground or to the belay stance. You should be familiar with self-rescue techniques. The basics are outlined below; but it is strongly recommended that you research these further and, most importantly, take the time to rehearse them under safe and controlled conditions.

➤ **Prussik knot:** fundamental to most self-rescue techniques is the prussik knot – or one of its derivatives. It is a self-tightening knot which when tied round another rope will grip it and hold a human's bodyweight. Even a free-hanging rope can be climbed using two prussik loops.

Each climber should carry at least two of these on their harness.

➤ **Getting out of the rope system:** if the fallen climber is unable to help himself, for instance: they're unconscious. Then the partner will need to tie them off – to stop them falling further – and then get out of the rope system to arrange a hoist and get help or assist them. To do this you will need to lock off the belay device, before

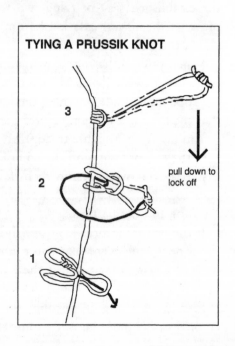

TYING A PRUSSIK KNOT

3

2

1

pull down to lock off

letting go of the rope to take further action. It's important to recognise that taking yourself out of the rope system is in itself a very risky thing to do on a climb. It should only be done in an emergency and the rescuer should make every attempt to belay themselves while effecting the rescue.

➤ **Assisted hoist:** an unconscious human is a remarkably heavy object and it's impossible to haul someone up with a rope if unassisted. If you can't lower them to safe ground you may need to hoist them up with an assisted hoist. To do this you will need

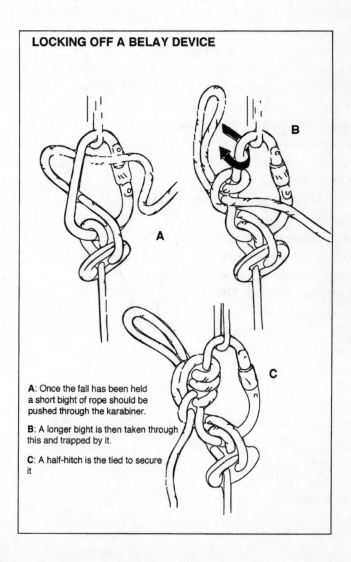

LOCKING OFF A BELAY DEVICE

A: Once the fall has been held a short bight of rope should be pushed through the karabiner.

B: A longer bight is then taken through this and trapped by it.

C: A half-hitch is the tied to secure it

to first tie them off using the method outlined previously. You can then rig a 'Z' hoist; this is the simplest of all the hoists but it will give you a mechanical advantage of 3:1 and allow you to lift the dead weight of your unconscious partner. It requires only the minimum of climbing gear, all of which should be readily at hand. It is also recommended that you have an emergency pulley on your rack, as this greatly reduces the friction over the karabiner. It isn't essential to have one to make the system work.

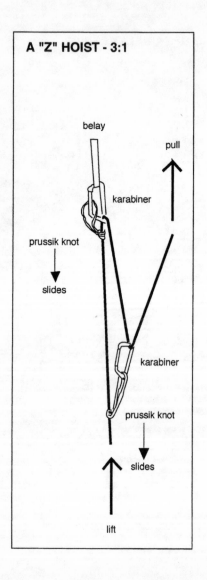

A "Z" HOIST - 3:1

belay

pull

karabiner

prussik knot

slides

karabiner

prussik knot

slides

lift

CONSERVATION AND ETHICS

It should be understood that our mountains and cliffs are a sensitive environment and that they are coming under an increasing amount pressure from those who seek to enjoy them. When compared with the activities of agriculture, industry and commerce, the effects upon them of mountaineers is small but, nevertheless, significant.

Increasingly, our activities as mountaineers are coming under the spotlight from both the government and other interested parties. We must play our part in setting a good example in helping to minimise our impact upon this precious resource. It should be simple enough to follow good habits, such as taking all waste home, but it is far often harder to take a detour to avoid breeding birds, or to opt to use public transport, rather than enjoying the convenience of our own cars. Perhaps car sharing is the best option. Nevertheless, we need to remain sensitive to the needs of the environment we have come to enjoy.

One area that is specific to climbing is the question of leader protection. Although the use of bolts for protection has been hotly debated for use on sports crags, the situation with regard to mountain crags has always been clear enough not to require debate. It is a time-honoured ethic – and one that is vital to the spirit of British climbing – that all protection used on the type of climb outlined in this book is traditional, leader placed, second removed and non-damaging devices.

Bolted protection is already starting to appear on many alpine trade routes; more often than not it is due to commercial pressure to get as many people up and down a route in as safe a manner as possible, rather than to the technical requirements of the climb. These same commercial pressures are starting to appear in the UK and are to the detriment of our climbing culture.

Finally, it must be understood that climbing, even when

established safety procedures are followed, is an inherently risk-based pursuit. While reasonable measures have been taken to establish the accuracy of the route descriptions in this book, they are, to some degree, a subjective interpretation. In addition, cliffs and crags do suffer from continual natural erosion that can alter – occasionally drastically – the nature of the terrain. Climbers needs to be prepared to make their own observations, assess risk, make appropriate decisions and be responsible for their own actions. On this basis, neither the author or the publisher accept any responsibility for any accident, loss or damage sustained while following any of the routes or procedures described in this book.

PART ONE

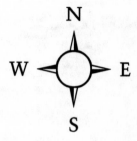

THE LAKE DISTRICT

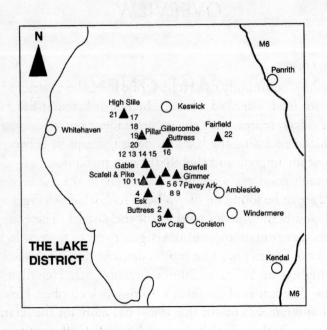

N

M6

Penrith

High Stile   Keswick
21 17
18
19 Pillar   Gillercombe   Fairfield
20   Buttress   22
Whitehaven
12 13 14 15   16

Gable   Bowfell
Scafell & Pike   Gimmer
10 11   5 6 7 Pavey Ark   Ambleside
4   8 9
Esk   1
Buttress   2   Windermere
3
Dow Crag   Coniston

THE LAKE
DISTRICT

Kendal

M6

OVERVIEW

GEOGRAPHY

The analogy commonly used to describe the Lake District and its mountains is of 'a spoked wheel'. The hub is based at Esk Hause and the ridges, representing the spokes, radiate outwards, with the dales, many enclosing the lakes acting as the gaps in between. It's a good, if incomplete and slightly skewed, metaphor.

Although good crags are found throughout the Lake District, the best are to be found on the volcanic rock which emerges in the central, southern and western part of the district. These are also the areas that contain most of the largest tracts of high, wild land.

The Lake District has four mountains over 3,000ft: Scafell Pike – the highest at 997m (3,206ft); Scafell Cliff; Helvellyn; and Skiddaw. The last is of no interest to the rock-climber; Helvellyn – fine mountaineer's massif that it is – has more for the scrambler and winter climber; Scafell Pike and Scafell Cliff continue as a mecca for climbers and remain a premier rock-climbing arena. But, as they say, size isn't everything, and other peaks such as Great Gable, Bowfell, Dow Crag and Pillar are equally rugged and shapely and provide great sport.

BACKGROUND

The influence of the Lakeland fells – a Norse term traditionally used in the district to name the mountains – and their crags on the history of mountaineering and rock-climbing far outweigh their modest size. And the activities of Lakeland cragsmen are writ equally large in any account of climbing's development.

Climbing on the area's cliffs was originally seen as a good practice for the Alps and the first routes were put up with the aim of reaching a summit. By the mid-1880s, however, the 'Alpine Golden Age' was past and our own cliffs started to be viewed as having their own worth. The ascent of Napes Needle in 1886 is accepted as the start of rock-climbing as a pursuit in its own right.

Following on from the establishment of the Climbers' Club in 1898 by the Welsh climbing fraternity – the first of the senior domestic climbing clubs – The Fell and Rock-Climbing Club was founded by Lakeland climbers in 1906.

For convenience, the routes are set out in this guide to follow the established division of fells, starting in the south-west and going around in a roughly clockwise direction.

APPROACHES

The south-east corner of the Lake District lies close to the M6 and is easy to reach. The main areas of interest for the climber, however, lie in the western part of the district and, with a few exceptions, involve a further drive of at least an hour or two after leaving the motorway. The most direct approaches tend to be through Ambleside or Keswick, but these invariably involve long drives along narrow, winding and frequently busy minor roads. A faster approach can be to take the A590/A595 and the A66 – roads that circumscribe the mountains and lead directly to the west coast. You can then cut back into the western dales spending less time on minor roads.

PUBLIC TRANSPORT

The closest you can get to the mountains by mainline train is to Windermere in the south; Penrith in the north; and Ravenglass and Whitehaven in the west. The Ravenglass–Eskdale miniature railway will take you part way up Eskdale; it is a very pleasant journey. There are some bus services – including the Mountain Goat Bus – into the dales from the railway stations, but they aren't, as yet, very frequent.

CENTRES

The major tourist centres are Ambleside and Keswick – and to a lesser extent Coniston and Cockermouth. They are all tourist traps, but you will find a good selection of equipment shops there. If you are staying overnight then it is better to stay closer to the mountains and into the dales proper. Langdale, Eskdale, Wasdale, Ennerdale, Buttermere, Borrowdale and Patterdale all have Youth Hostels, campsites and pubs.

1. ARÊTE, CHIMNEY AND CRACK

Mountain: Dow Crag (883m).

Cliff: 'A' Buttress.

Location: GR: 264997.

Grade: Mild Severe.

Height: 97m.

Time: 3–5 hrs.

Parking: Walna Scar Road; GR: 289970

Maps: OS Outdoor Leisure (1:25000)
   sheet 6, OS Landranger (1:50000)
   sheets 96 & 97; Harvey's (1:25000 &

1:40000) Southern Lakeland.

Guidebook: F&RCC – Dow, Duddon and
   Slate.

Equipment: 2 x 9mm ropes; a
   comprehensive rack with small to
   medium-sized placements and at least
   3 full-length slings.

Accommodation: Coniston Coppermines
   YH; tel: (01539) 441261.

INTRODUCTION
Of all of Dow Crag's cliffs, 'A' Buttress is the most complete and self-contained. Its sound and compact rock soars magnificently from the scree to a well-defined summit and all its faces are steep. The routes on it have a degree of technical difficulty and a lot of exposure.

Arête, Chimney and Crack follow a crafty but entirely logical line that makes best use of 'A' Buttress's features. While it is the easiest route on the face, the climbing is always varied and often quite technical. It always maintains a sense of interest and provides excitement as well.

SITUATION
'A' Buttress is the only one of Dow Crag's Buttresses to provide continuous climbing from base to summit. As you look at the crag, it is the prominent buttress at the left-hand side of the cliff which is bounded on the left by Easy Gully and South Rake. To the right is Great Gully.

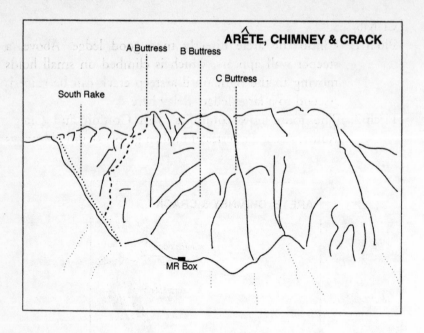

Arête, Chimney and Crack share its middle pitches – including the all-important high-level traverse – with Gordon and Craig's Route. Nevertheless, both routes retain a highly individual character and both have sensational finishes.

APPROACH

Follow the Walna Scar road through the two prominent 'rock gates' and on to the large cairn in view of the footbridge over Torver Beck. Turn right at the cairn and follow the path up the bank and on up and over the lip below Goat's Water. At the tarn's outflow, cross the stream and head up the screes to the base of the crag – the Mountain Rescue box is a good reference point.

From the box turn left and skirt around the base of the crag, past Great Gully and on to where South Rake cuts in from the left. At the left-hand base of the buttress, a well-defined arête, complete with quartz streaks, can be seen. This is the arête of Arête, Chimney and Crack.

CLIMB

Pitch 1: Climb the arête directly to a good ledge. Above, a steeper wall appears, which is climbed on small holds moving to the right until a steep crack can be gained. Ascend to a large ledge. Belay here.

Pitch 2: The route now combines with Gordon and Craig's Route. Ascend a series of broken grooves-cum-chimneys

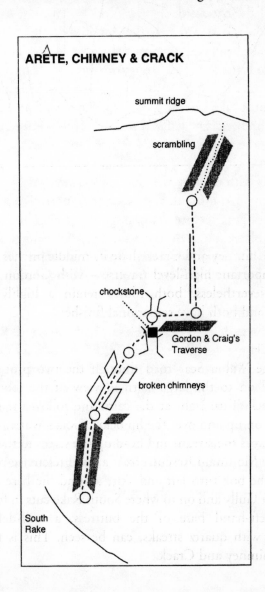

that trend to the right. This leads to a recess complete with an obvious pinnacle for a belay. Belay here.

Pitch 3: The groove line continues, but gives way to a series of flakes that, in turn, lead to a major chimney, topped off by a large chockstone. Bridge the chimney and then climb the chockstone direct. The holds are good and the overhang is easily dealt with by bridging. Belay on top of the chockstone.

Pitch 4: You can now access Gordon and Craig's traverse. This ledge leads right across the upper section of the buttress and although it's straightforward the exposure is awesome. It can be readily protected for the leader but you must take care in protecting the second and subsequent climbers. The ledge is split by a pronounced crack. This is the final pitch but you need to go beyond it to belay in a niche.

Pitch 5: As with the traverse, this crack is awesomely exposed but isn't that difficult and can be well protected. Climb it by bridging before 'jamming' the crack. It leads to an isolated pinnacle connected to the main mountainside by a narrow arête. Straightforward, if exposed, scrambling will see you to Dow Crag's summit ridge.

DESCENT

The most direct descent lies to the south, down South Rake; if you opt for this route don't be taken in at the top of Easy Gully – as it leads to difficult ground – and make sure you clear the summit of Easy Buttress before descending. The remainder of the Coniston Fells can be easily accessed from Dow Crag via Goat's Hause. One option is to head for the summit of Coniston Old Man and descend from Levers Hawse to Levers Water and then pick up the track that cuts through Boulder Valley and back to the Walna Scar road.

2. GIANT'S CRAWL

Mountain: Dow Crag (883m).
Cliff: 'B' Buttress.
Location: GR: 263976.
Grade: Difficult.
Height: 125m.
Time: 3–5 hrs.
Parking: Walna Scar Road; GR: 289970.
Maps: OS Outdoor Leisure (1:25000) sheet 6; OS Landranger (1:50000) sheet 96; Harvey's Map (1:25000 or 1:40000) Southern Lakeland.
Guidebook: F&RCC – Dow, Duddon and Slate.
Equipment: 2 x 9mm ropes; a rack including small to medium placements; at least three full-length slings.
Accommodation: Coniston Coppermines YH; tel: (01539) 441261

INTRODUCTION

Giant's Crawl follows the most obvious line on 'B' Buttress. Found on the cliff's left-hand upper section, it's an uncompromising ramp that cleaves the crag from lower left to upper right. It's a good natural line but very exposed. The buttress doesn't lead all the way to the summit ridge but this climb seeks out the best of the broken rock above to lead to Dow's summit ridge.

Although the route is technically straightforward, it is very exposed. Both a lead and second climber would be likely to suffer a possibly fatal pendulum if they came off and hadn't taken due care with their protection. The rock is also heavily pockmarked with quartz; when dry it provides great holds, but when wet it seems like ice.

SITUATION

'B' Buttress is the second from the left of Dow Crag's major buttresses. A large, dome-shaped rock that – although falling short of the summit ridge – is one of the mountain's major supporting

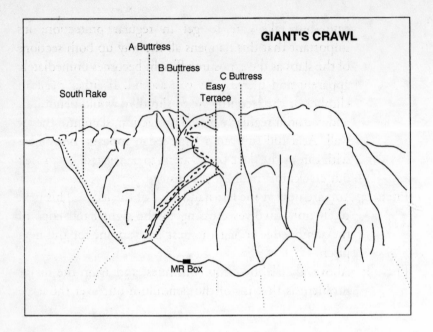

features. Defined on the left by Great Gully and on the right by Easy Terrace.

It's split into an upper and lower section by the gully and enclosing arête that forms Easy Terrace. Giant's Crawl is located on the upper section and is the slabby ramp that runs parallel to – and above – Easy Terrace. The ramp comes to an end and bisects the southern extension of Easy Terrace a good 100m short of the summit ridge; then the climb branches off left and seeks out continuous rock above the main buttress and on the edge of Great Gully.

APPROACH
See *1 Arête, Chimney and Crack*. From the Mountain Rescue box turn left and follow the base of the crag to the bottom of Easy Terrace. Go beyond the terrace to the next gully and then look immediately behind to see the slabby ramp of Giant's Crawl.

CLIMB
Pitch 1:   A wall leads directly to the base of the first set of slabs and the bottom of the massive ramp. Climb this part with

ease, but take care to get in regular protection; it's important that this happens all the way up both sections of the slabs as the exposure off right becomes immediately apparent and increases as you ascend. If either the lead climber or the second were to slip they would pendulum and, without regularly placed protection, slam into the far wall. At a full run-out a large ledge appears. Belay here with care as the flake belays aren't to be trusted; try to seek out cracks for small 'Rocks' instead.

Pitch 2: You are now at the left-hand edge of the ledge. This next pitch only involves crossing to the right-hand edge of the same ledge to get the best belay point for the next pitch.

Pitch 3: Above, the slabby ramp continues, and again the major problem is the risk of the pendulum out over the large

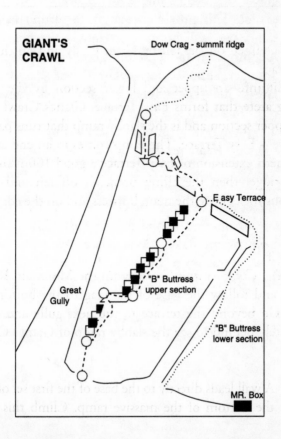

chasm to the right. The going is actually very pleasant with a grand feeling of exposure. There is no shortage of good placements, however, so you can manage the risk. Take care of the quartz at mid-height. Just beyond the quartz, the ramp narrows and you will really feel 'out there'. Concentrate on good placements. Another large ledge appears but, once again, you'll need to seek out the belay points carefully.

Pitch 4: More of the same until you reach Easy Terrace. Belay here.

Pitch 5: The main section of the climb is now over and many climbers traverse left to descend down Easy Terrace. If you opt for this keep the rope on as there is one exposed move as you cross the top of the chimney that forms the left-hand side of the terrace. By traversing left along a grassy ledge you come across a problematic, but short, corner. This provides access to a second ledge and a stance perched above Great Gully. Belay here.

Pitch 6: A committing move around a corner leads to the base of a longer, although less-awkward, crack. Situated above Great Gully, the moves are exposed but enjoyable. Exit right to a belay at a ledge.

Pitch 7: Climbing now gives way to scrambling and the summit ridge is rapidly reached.

DESCENT

The most direct descent route is to clear both 'A' and Easy Buttress – don't start to descend at the top of Easy Gully – and then descend down South Rake. Good fell walking can be had by connecting with the main Coniston Fells via Goat's Hause as described in *1 Arête, Chimney and Crack*.

3. 'C' ORDINARY

Mountain: Dow Crag (883m).

Cliff: 'C' Buttress.

Location: GR: 263977.

Grade: Difficult.

Height: 110m.

Time: 3–5 hrs.

Parking: Walna Scar Road; GR: 289970.

Maps: OS Outdoor Leisure (1:25000)
   sheet 6; OS Landranger (1:50000)
   sheet 96; Harvey's Map (1:25000 or

1:40000) Southern Lakeland.

Guidebook: F&RCC – Dow, Duddon and
   Slate.

Equipment: 2 x 9mm ropes; a rack
   including small to medium placements
   and a large hexcentric; at least three
   full-length slings.

Accommodation: Coniston Coppermines
   YH; tel: (01539) 441261.

INTRODUCTION

'C' Ordinary is the traditional introduction to – and often the first lead on – Dow Crag. It fulfils both these roles admirably and delivers just enough excitement and variation to make the experience satisfying. Its one drawback is that the buttress falls well short of the summit ridge. It can, however, be extended by using the upper section of Easy Terrace to clear the top of Central Chimney and give access to a scramble up and on to Dow Crag's summit ridge.

SITUATION

'C' Buttress is the third from the left of Dow Crag's major buttresses. It's a well-defined pinnacle bordered by Central Chimney on the left and Intermediate Gully on the right. A domed slab is apparent at two-thirds of the height. The rock is very sound – if well polished – but can be treacherous in the wet.

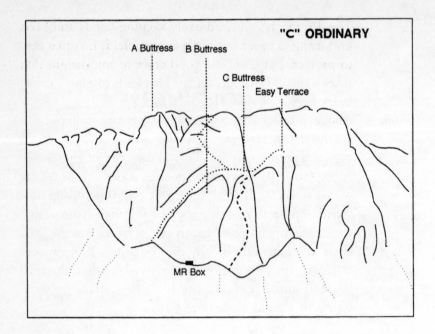

APPROACH

See *1 Arête, Chimney and Crack*. From the Mountain Rescue box turn right, skirt around the bottom of 'B' Buttress and clear Central Chimney. You are now at the bottom of 'C' Buttress. Go to its lowest point; above is a broad, slabby rib. 'C' Ordinary climbs this.

CLIMB

Pitch 1: The rib can be climbed easily, and pretty much at will. It's broken up into a series of short walls by several ledges. You should keep an eye out for good protection – it's there but it isn't over-abundant. A full run-out leads to a good belay ledge below a pronounced steepening.

Pitch 2: Go to the left-hand end of the ledge and climb a series of shallow grooves. These will lead you out on to an exposed position over Central Gully; the holds come readily to hand and the protection is sound. A series of ledges and small slabs leads to the base of the large domed slab. Belay here.

Pitch 3: The domed slab is one of the highlights of the climb.

Trend right; it's climbed easily keeping hands and heels low, using as much boot sole as possible. It isn't that easy to protect, but there is a good crack at mid-height that takes a small 'Rock' or similar. This leads to a large ledge. Belay here.

Pitch 4: Above, a series of flakes leads off left and they provide a semi hand traverse. They are followed by a much bigger flake-cum-spike. This is the crux of the climb. A big (size 10) Hexcentric goes in a treat around here – you'll certainly feel the need for something substantial. The flake can either be climbed from inside the crack or, more elegantly, by a hand traverse and then a mantleshelf on the outside. Be warned, however, the latter option is only viable when the rock is clean and dry. From the top of the flake you can climb to a good niche. Belay here.

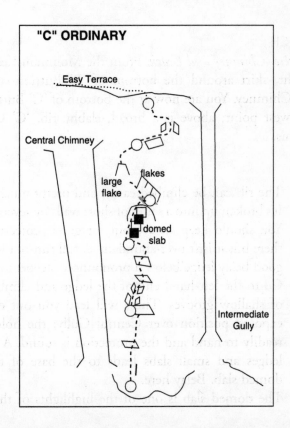

Pitch 5: A ramp leads off left, around a corner, up a short arête and then back on itself. This leads to Easy Terrace.

SCRAMBLE
The usual climbers' descent lies off to the left along Easy Terrace. Once Central Chimney is cleared, an arête that forms the left-hand side of a gully leads down to the base of the crag. The route uses both the edge of the arête and the gully.

To do the scramble, clear Easy Terrace's descent route and then continue traversing along the southern extension of the terrace. There is one exposed step to clear, so it's worth keeping the rope on. From the top of Giant's Crawl, you can then cut back to the right and follow a rising traverse over broken rocks to the summit.

DESCENT
See *1 Arête, Chimney and Crack.*

4. BRIDGER'S ROUTE

Mountain: Scafell Pike (978m).

Cliff: Esk Buttress (shown on some maps as Dow Crag).

Location: GR: 223065.

Grade: Hard Severe.

Height: 71m.

Time: 6+ hrs.

Parking: Lay-bys at foot of Hard Knott Pass; GR: 213011.

Maps: OS Outdoor Leisure (1:25000) sheet 6, OS Landranger (1:50000) sheets 96 & 97; Harvey's Maps (1:25000 & 1:40000) Western Lakeland.

Guidebook: F&RCC – Scafell, Wasdale & Eskdale.

Equipment: 2 x 9mm ropes; a comprehensive rack with small to medium placements and at least three full-length slings.

Accommodation: Eskdale YH; tel: (01946) 723219.

INTRODUCTION

Upper Eskdale cuts deep into the central hub of the Lakeland mountains; it's a wild, remote and lonely place that has no equals in the district. The surrounding mountains – England's highest – are superb. The dale is dominated by the Great Moss and, in particular, by Esk Buttress. The latter is an isolated and very impressive cliff; and, in sympathy with its position, all of its climbs are serious propositions. Bridger's Route, although following a traversing line, goes straight through the exposed rock of the crag's Central Pillar and – despite an interesting relationship with the dramatic Red Edge – is the most straightforward line on the cliff.

Bridger's Route is an intricate and exposed climb involving some quite-technical climbing. It well deserves its classic status; the cliff tends to inspire awe – particularly on first acquaintance. There's also a good chance that the crag will be quieter than most in the Lakes, so you'll be able to relish the solitude.

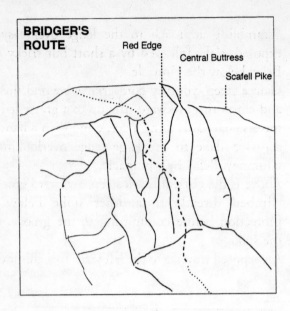

SITUATION
Esk Buttress looms over Upper Eskdale and the Great Moss and forms a lower bastion of Scafell Pike's eastern flank. The cliff rises from the remarkable expanse of the Great Moss and culminates in the Central Pillar – its highest point. It is defined to the north by Little Narrowcove and to the south by Cam Spout.

APPROACH
All ways into Esk Buttress are long. While this isn't the shortest or the most direct route, it is the most straightforward. Leave the road and follow the marked track through Brotherilkeld and on up into Upper Eskdale. The path is easy to follow. Take the left-hand fork at Lingcove Bridge and continue on alongside the River Esk and across the Great Moss. Esk Buttress will now be apparent and is approached over scree and then slabs.

To identify Bridger's Route, first locate the pronounced Square Chimney, on the left of the Central Pillar area. This is on the steep wall above the broken rock and the easy, angled slabs at the base of the cliffs. Look down and to the right, and you will be able to see a square ledge below a detached pillar. This is the start of the climb proper and can only be reached after a scramble.

CLIMB

Pitch 1: Scrambling approach to the ledge over easy, though exposed, slabs followed by a short but tricky chimney. Belay below the pinnacle.

Pitch 2: Gain a steep chimney-cum-groove beyond the pinnacle and climb this awkward part up to a grassy ledge. Then traverse leftwards using a crack and then a hand traverse across a flake to the large ledge overlooking Square Chimney. Belay by a pinnacle.

Pitch 3: Above is the crux; this is a steep, awkward groove and is climbed directly to another spike belay. Arrange protection before committing to the groove. Belay by the spike.

Pitch 4: An exposed traverse to the left leads to a chimney. Climb

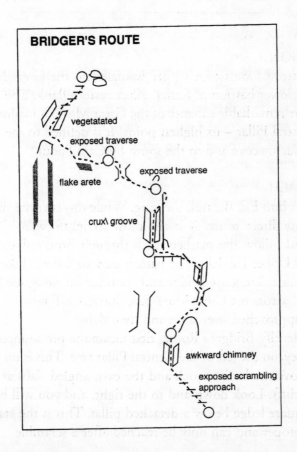

this using a groove on the left to gain yet another spike belay.

Pitch 5: Continue traversing left to gain the edge of the buttress by a series of flakes. The going remains exposed but less technical. Climb the flakes to a vegetated groove – this is climbed direct and leads to exposed scrambling and the top. Belay by a prominent block.

DESCENT

For a direct descent, move well back from the buttress and pick up a faint path that heads north – going below Pen – and then pick up the Little Narrowcove path. This leads back to the Great Moss and the base of the Buttress.

From the top of Esk Buttress you are well placed to take in the summit of Scafell Pike via a grade-three scramble on Pen. From the top of Esk Buttress go back and pick up the descent path. Identify Pen from this and then go to the left-hand side of the rocks.

A groove which breaks through the full height of the initial steep rock step can be readily seen. This is climbed – and belayed – and leads to a slab, which, following an awkward step, leads to easier ground and the lonely summit of Pen.

Continue north-west over broken ground for a kilometre until you reach the summit of Scafell Pike. It's probably been quite a long day by now; so a direct return is called for. From the summit cairn head south-west down to Mickledore, before dropping down off the ridge before Broad Stand and the cut down to Cam Spout and the Great Moss. It's still quite a long walk, but the scenery is magnificent.

5. CRESCENT SLABS AND GWYNNE'S CHIMNEY

Mountain: Pavey Ark (702m).
Cliff: Pavey Ark.
Location: GR: 285079.
Grade: Mild Severe and Very Difficult.
Height: 85m.
Time: 3–5 hrs.
Parking: New Dungeon Ghyll Hotel; GR: 296064.
Maps: OS Outdoor Leisure (1:25000) sheet 6, OS Landranger (1:50000)
sheets 96 & 97; Harvey's Maps (1:25000 &1:40000) Centre Lakeland.
Guidebook: F&RCC – Langdale.
Equipment: Either an 11mm or 2 x 9mm ropes; a comprehensive rack with full range of placements and at least three full-length slings.
Accommodation: Elterwater YH; tel: (01539) 437245.

INTRODUCTION

That Pavey Ark is an impressive cliff is never in doubt, but, at first acquaintance, it doesn't appear that inviting. The rock looks very vegetated, loose and damp. Fortunately, the reality is much more accommodating, and the rock is actually quite sound and possesses remarkably fine friction.

Given that the cliff is split in two by Jack's Rake, no single climb ascends the crag's central area. Crescent Slabs and Gwynne's Chimney, however, can be connected to provide a remarkably direct line. Despite being of a diverse nature, they both provide challenging, enjoyable and uncomplicated climbing, taking you high on to this fine cliff and to a great summit.

SITUATION

Pavey Ark rises directly over Stickle Tarn and looks a very daunting cliff. Its most remarkable feature is Jack's Rake, a ledge that follows

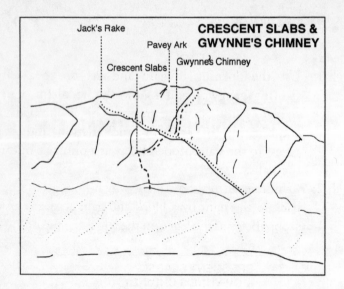

a rising traverse from lower right to upper left, providing both a climbers' descent and a very popular scramble. The cliff is defined on the left by Little Gully and on the right by East Gully.

The cliff below Jack's Rake is compact and has two prominent features: Stony Buttress and Crescent Slabs – the latter is named for a crescent-shaped corner that forms its left-hand edge. Below the slab is a steepening overhang known as the Barrier.

Above Jack's Rake the rock is less compact and is broken into pronounced chimneys and arêtes. Gwynne's Chimney is prominent and leads directly to the summit.

APPROACH

The approach is short and simple – the biggest problem is avoiding the crowds on a summer weekend. Make your way through the New Dungeon Ghyll Hotel complex and follow the signs for Stickle Ghyll. Follow the heavily eroded path up to Stickle Tarn.

From the dam cut around the tarn and then follow the path over the screes to the lower, right-hand end of Jack's Rake. Skirt below the rocks of the Barrier until an opening of stained black rock appears by a pronounced bulge towards the right of the slabs.

1. Crescent Slabs

CLIMB

Pitch 1: Use the opening to gain and get on to a leftward-slanting gangway and follow this for 12m. Cut back right to gain a shallow groove. This is climbed using a combination of bridging and friction and provides access to the slabs proper. Belay at a pinnacle midway up the slabs.

Pitch 2: Continue on up the slabs – which now get steeper. Cut back to the right by a block and gain access to a shallow scoop. Belay at the ledge on the left at the top of the scoop.

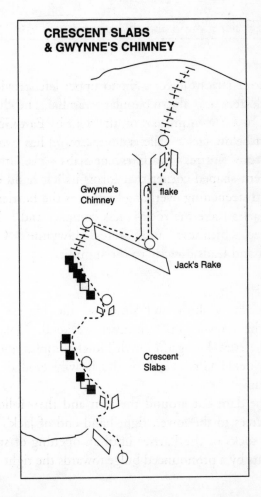

CRESCENT SLABS
& GWYNNE'S CHIMNEY

Gwynne's
Chimney

flake

Jack's Rake

Crescent
Slabs

Pitch 3: From here it's simply a matter of padding up pleasantly angled slabs to gain the Crescent and then on to Jack's Rake. Scramble down Jack's Rake for a short distance, over the rock step and locate a prominent chimney; this is Gwynne's Chimney.

2. Gwynne's Chimney

CLIMB
Pitch 1: Go into the chimney and climb directly by bridging moves. At a pronounced flake within the chimney, exit right out on to the open face of a blunt arête that leads to easier ground and the summit.

DESCENT
To descend via Jack's Rake, go west to clear the summit plateau. As you start dropping down, some rough slabs appear by a dry stone wall; a cairn confirms the route. Drop down the slabs to the upper entrance of Jack's Rake and scramble down an obvious ledge-and-ramp system. Pick up the outward path.

6. MIDDLEFELL BUTTRESS

Mountain: Langdale Pikes (736m).

Cliff: Middlefell Buttress.

Location: GR: 285064.

Grade: Difficult.

Height: 75m.

Time: 2–3hrs.

 d Dungeon Ghyll Hotel; GR:

tdoor Leisure (1:25000)

Landranger (1:50000)

sheets 89 or 90; Harvey's Map (1:25000 or 1:40000) Centre Lakeland.

Guidebook: F&RCC – Langdale.

Equipment: Either an 11mm or 2 x 9mm rope; a rack that has small to medium placements; at least three full-length slings.

Accommodation: Elterwater YH; tel: (01539) 437245.

...uttress, the name of both the climb and the cliff, is a very straightforward route that gets you out of the enclosures of Langdale and on to the heights. It's the least painful approach to Gimmer and is readily combined with a route on that superb cliff.

Middlefell Buttress is a good route in its own right and can be attempted in all but the worst conditions. It's a frequent introduction climb and is an ideal first lead. The climbing may be straightforward but it's always engrossing with just the right level of exposure.

SITUATION
Middlefell Buttress rises directly out of the Langdale Valley, above the Old Dungeon Ghyll Hotel, and forms the lower bastion of the Langdale Pikes. It's the left-hand and highest buttress of Raven Crag, from which it is separated by Raven Crag Gully.

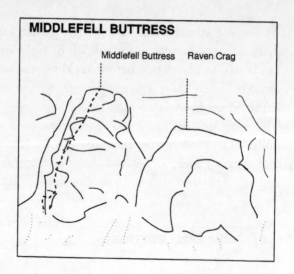

MIDDLEFELL BUTTRESS

Middlefell Buttress   Raven Crag

APPROACH

The approach is straightforward and follows the obvious zigzags up the scree behind the Old Dungeon Ghyll Hotel. Middlefell Buttress – the climb – follows the left-hand edge of Middlefell Buttress – the crag. A good reference point is the anti-erosion fence by the bottom left of the buttress. Above this is a detached pinnacle; go beyond this into the gully to the chimney that separates the pinnacle from the main crag.

CLIMB

Pitch 1:   Climb the chimney behind the pinnacle, then gain its top before scrambling on to a large ledge. Belay here.

Pitch 2:   From this comfortable belay – these are a feature of the entire climb – look to a large, quite steep wall that seems to go on and on. You will be able to make out a rising traverse going bottom right to take you on to the left-hand edge of the buttress. Follow this and keep going upwards for a full run-out. The climbing is delightfully straightforward with obvious holds, exhilarating exposure and abundant protection. Don't be seduced by its easy nature: it's a long drop, and the potential for a slip is always there. Seek out and use the placements for protection. This long pitch leads to another large ledge.

Pitch 3: Above is a steeper wall that at first glance looks quite demanding. The trick is to look left or right and use the holds off to the flank before tackling the steep rock directly. Then there are good holds to the top of the climb where there is another large ledge.

Pitch 4: The usual descent lies off to the left and leads down the gully. The climb can be extended to gain further height and then a good path that leads to Gimmer Crag; look to your right and you will see that another pitch can be

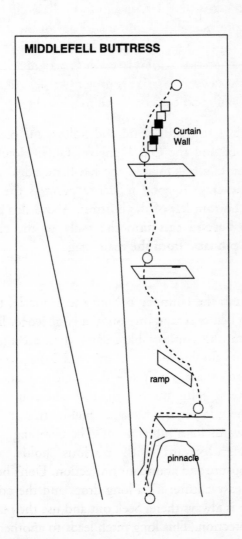

climbed from the buttress. A steepish slab can be seen which holds a rising traverse from left to right and will give another 20m of climbing at a grade of Difficult. The route is known as Curtain Wall. As is often the case with a slab, the rock is compact and getting protection in requires good observation. Smaller size 'Rocks' and 'Super Rocks' are recommended.

DESCENT

For a direct descent head left and pick up the gully mentioned in Pitch 4. To continue on to Gimmer, or one of the Langdale Pikes summits, head on up an open hillside which has small outcrops. Make your way up this until it levels out and you reach a path that trends roughly east to west. This provides access to the Langdale Pikes, and also a good traverse to Gimmer Crag, by heading west for 400m. See 7 *Gimmer Chimney*.

7. GIMMER CHIMNEY

Mountain: Pike of Stickle (709m).
Cliff: South-east Face of Gimmer Crag.
Location: GR: 278069.
Grade: Very Difficult.
Height: 90m.
Time: 3–5 hrs.
Parking: Old Dungeon Ghyll Hotel; GR: 286061.
Maps: OS Outdoor Leisure (1:25000) sheet 6; OS Landranger (1:50000) sheet 89 or 90; Harvey's Map (1:25000 or 1:40000) Centre Lakeland.
Guidebook: F&RCC – Langdale.
Equipment: Either an 11mm or 2 x 9mm rope and a rack including a full range of placements and at least three full-length slings.
Accommodation: Elterwater YH; tel: (01539) 437245.

INTRODUCTION

Gimmer Crag is without doubt Langdale's finest crag – a bold statement considering the competition. It stands proud over the northern slopes of Mickleden and, although it doesn't directly support a summit, its closest neighbour is Pike of Stickle – a particularly spectacular summit. It also has a remarkable concentration of high-quality climbs; many in the lower and middle grade.

Gimmer Chimney is the most obvious feature on the crag's south-eastern flank and is the most obvious way up the cliff. It follows a continuous line from the base to the summit of the crag. A highly satisfying climb, it's well graded but is no pushover and it has a high level of exposure.

SITUATION

Gimmer Crag emerges from the open fellside and stands complete, compact and isolated. The crag is barrel- or half-barrel-shaped and is a complex cliff. The rock is bounded on the right by

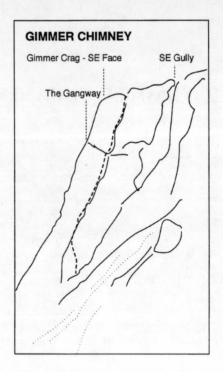

South-east Gully and the South-east Face – the crag's major aspect rises directly above this. Ash Tree Ledges impinges from the left, but doesn't break up the continuous sweep of this face. The line of Gimmer Chimney is broken only once – at mid-height by the Gangway – where it closes in with its famous neighbour, Bracket and Slab.

APPROACH

If, as suggested in *6 Middlefell Buttress*, you approach Gimmer Crag from the top of Middlefell Buttress you will save yourself a brutally direct ascent up from the valley floor. From the top of the buttress it's simply a matter of gaining and following a fairly level path that traverses the hillside. This leads round to the base of the crag.

If you don't go via Middlefell Buttress, you are left with two approaches: the first is from the Mickleden path and leads directly up the hillside; the second is to head up the Raven Crag path then leave this next to a stone bridge. The left-hand fork leads to some steep zigzags and a direct approach to the base of the crag.

To locate the climb find and gain Easy Gully and then locate South-east Gully – the crag's right-hand boundary – then look left to a deep chimney. This is Gimmer Chimney.

CLIMB

Pitch 1: From Easy Gully gain a groove that leads to the base of a rib. Belay here.

Pitch 2: Climb the rib directly and easily. Belay at the base of the chimney.

Pitch 3: Now for a more serious pitch. Climb the chimney easily and then up a much more taxing crack. Rig your protection before you commit to this. Belay at the top of the crack.

Pitch 4: A delicate traverse left for three metres leads to a shallow

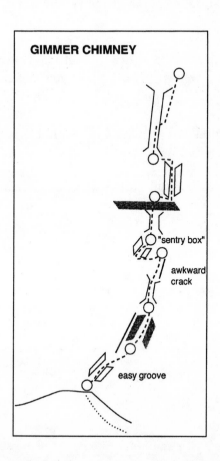

GIMMER CHIMNEY

and awkward corner. Rig some protection and then climb this directly to the sentry box belay.

Pitch 5: You leave the sentry box by way of a chimney-cum-crack. Use the right-hand wall to gain access to a large ledge called the Gangway. Belay here.

Pitch 6: Two chimneys-cum-cracks leave the Gangway; the left-hand one is the crux of the Bracket and Slab, so avoid this unless you want a real Hard Severe thrutch of a move. The one on the right-hand belongs to Gimmer Chimney – although you might come across the odd 'refugee' from Bracket and Slab – and is straightforward. Belay above and to the left of this.

Pitch 7: The final pitch starts off in an easy-to-climb chimney, this is then left at half height for an equally accommodating but exposed rib. Follow this to the top.

DESCENT

The climbers' descent lies off to the right and then down South-east Gully; it's a well-polished trail. If you want a summit then head north beyond the gully and pick up the path that leads to Pike of Stickle.

From the uphill side it's a simple scramble to gain the Lake District's most recognisable top. A good walk from here is to head north-west over Martcrag Moor and to descend into upper Mickleden via Stake Gill and then back to the Old Dungeon Ghyll Hotel.

8. ASH TREE SLABS AND 'D' ROUTE

Mountain: Pike of Stickle (709m).

Cliff: Lower North-west Face and the West Face of Gimmer Crag.

Location: GR: 278069.

Grade: Very Difficult and Severe.

Height: 50m & 35m.

Time: 3–5 hrs.

Parking: Old Dungeon Ghyll Hotel; GR: 286061.

Maps: OS Outdoor Leisure (1:25000) sheet 6; OS Landranger (1:50000) sheet 89 or 90; Harvey's Map (1:25000 or 1:40000) Centre Lakeland.

Guidebook: F&RCC – Langdale.

Equipment: Either an 11mm or 2 x 9mm rope and a rack including a full range of placements and at least three full-length slings.

Accommodation: Elterwater YH; tel: (01539) 437245.

INTRODUCTION

Gimmer Crag's Mickleden Face is without doubt one of the best rock faces in the Lake District and has a multitude of great climbs. The one disappointment is that large parts of it are broken at two-thirds height by Ash Tree Ledges and no single route ascends the complete face.

This is a minor distraction, however, and it is relatively easy to connect any number of great climbs for a complete ascent. Given that the most important feature on the face is Ash Tree Slabs it makes sense to look to this. A fine climb of the same name tackles them at a comfortable grade of Very Difficult.

Above Ash Tree Ledges are Gimmer's famous and alphabetically listed West Face classics: 'A', 'B', 'C', 'D', 'E' and 'F'. With the exception of 'F' they are all rated between a good Very Difficult and an equally good Hard Severe. All provide fine onward climbing to the top of the crag, although 'D' probably has the best reputation.

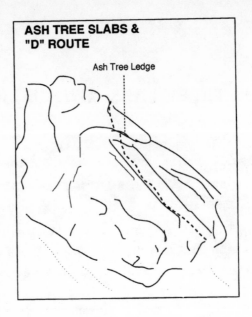

ASH TREE SLABS &
"D" ROUTE

Ash Tree Ledge

SITUATION

To the west of the South-east Face (see *7 Gimmer Chimney*) is a collection of smaller walls known collectively as the Mickleden Face. This is split by Ash Tree Ledges into the West Face (which lies above the ledges); the Lower North-west Face (which lies below the ledges); and the North-west Face (which isn't reached by the ledges and is fairly complete).

The Lower North-west Face is dominated by Ash Tree Corner and Ash Tree Slabs. The West Face rises directly from Ash Tree Ledges and consists of compact rock broken by defined features; 'D' route follows a superb crack system up this.

APPROACH

See *7 Gimmer Chimney*. To locate the climb, skirt around the base of the rock to the clearing of Easy Gully and locate an obvious detached flake to the left of the crag's lowest point. Ash Tree Corner and then Ash Tree Slabs lie to the left of this.

1. Ash Tree Slabs

CLIMB

Pitch 1:   Ascend the first three metres of Ash Tree Corner before reaching a rising traverse out on the left which leads on to the slabs and up on to the exposed edge of the slab. It's great climbing, but look to your protection as, with any slab, there isn't an overabundance of placements. Belay on a good ledge.

Pitch 2:   Continue up the edge to gain a groove that cuts back

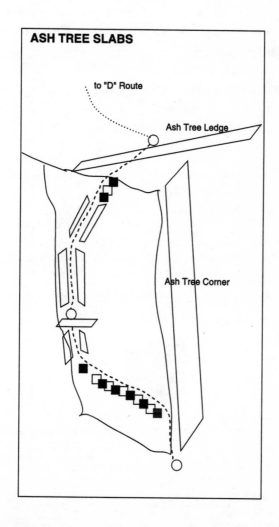

right to gain the upper slab. Continue up the slab to Ash Tree Ledges and belay here.

2. 'D' Route

CLIMB

Scramble up the ledges, initially to the left but then to the right, to gain the uppermost ledge. Go to the right-hand end of this and find a large block to the right of some very compact slabs.

Pitch 1: A chimney rises out of a recess; this is easily climbed but is followed by a tricky traverse between some bulges to gain access to a right slating crack. Climb this to a ledge to an optional belay.

Pitch 2: Continue up the crack to below the final overhangs. Here you need to move right to gain a groove that breaks through the upper wall. Look to your protection and climb boldly through this. Belay at the top.

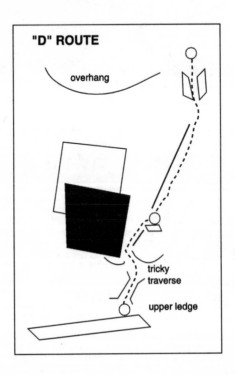

DESCENT

The climbers' descent is gained by heading right to clear Junipall Gully – this can be descended but isn't recommended. It is better to clear this and reach a vegetated spur which provides access to a path which then cuts back to the base of the crag.

As with *7 Gimmer Chimney*, the logical summit is Pike of Stickle.

9. BOWFELL BUTTRESS

Mountain: Bow Fell (902m).
Cliff: Bowfell Buttress.
Location: GR: 245066.
Grade: Difficult.
Height: 106m.
Time: 4–5hrs.
Parking: Old Dungeon Ghyll Hotel car
park; GR: 286061.
Maps: OS Outdoor Leisure (1:25000)
sheet 6; OS Landranger (1:50000)
sheet 89 or 90; Harvey's Map
(1:25000 or 1:40000) Centre
Lakeland.
Guidebook: F&RCC – Langdale.
Equipment: Either an 11mm or 2 x 9mm
rope and a rack including a full range
of placements and at least three full-
length slings.
Accommodation: Elterwater YH; tel:
(01539) 437245.

INTRODUCTION

Bow Fell and Bowfell Buttress dominate Mickleden and the head of Langdale. A well-defined summit supported by an impressive cliff, it more than hold its own in what is one of the best known and most impressive skylines in Britain.

Although the route is only graded as Difficult – and many have questioned this on its real thrutch of a crux – it's the most direct line on the cliff. It follows a perpendicular line from just about the lowest point of the crag to its summit. It has rightly maintained its classic status for many years.

SITUATION

Bow Fell towers over Mickleden, the most westerly offshoot of Langdale. Bowfell Buttress dominates the mountain's eastern flank. The mountain is defined to the south by the high col atop the Band, and in the north by an equally high col, Ore Gap.

Bowfell Buttress is the culmination of the crags and steep scree that rises directly above Mickleden. It stands aloof at the boundary between the green of the dale and the largest and highest tract of of mountainous country in the Lake District.

APPROACH

From the Old Dungeon Ghyll Hotel follow the farm track that leads to Stool End and the base of the Band. A well-trodden path leads up this and should be followed to GR: 251062. Here a second path branches off north-west and traverses across the hillside below Flat Crag and Cambridge Buttress to the base of Bowfell Buttress. Head for the lowest part of the crag.

CLIMB

Pitch 1: Just left of centre of the bottom of Bowfell Buttress is the lowest point from where you should be able to identify a ridge. This is climbed easily. At a half run-out, a chimney can be seen trending high right. This has smooth sides but can be climbed to gain a good ledge. Belay here.

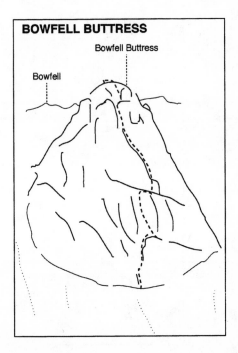

Pitch 2: A short slab-cum-wall trends left; climb this to gain a chimney – which can be ascended directly and leads to a large ledge. Traverse along this for about eight metres until you reach the bottom of an obvious crack. Belay here.

Pitch 3: This is the notorious Difficult Crack. For a short section you'll be climbing above the climb's given grade, but its reputation has probably grown a bit beyond reality. It's a thrutch but can be readily protected and is soon over. It probably makes sense to place your protection and then retire, before climbing it in one continuous move. The rock is steep, and weight will be on your arms. With determination, rather than grace, you'll soon be able to flop on to a ledge. The crux is now behind but you'll still

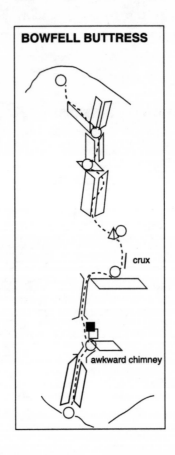

BOWFELL BUTTRESS

crux

awkward chimney

feel out an a limb as you climb the slabs in a rising traverse to the left. A welcome belay appears at an obvious pinnacle. Belay here.

Pitch 4: Off to the left is a groove that leads into a chimney. Climb this, directly at first, then cut out right at a ledge on to the wall. Continue up this for six metres until you can see a large ledge, complete with a fine pinnacle belay. A long and committing stretch left is required to gain it. Belay here.

Pitch 5: Go back into the chimney until you can gain a left trending ramp, this leads in a rising traverse to easy ground and the top of the climb.

DESCENT

The summit of Bowfell Buttress stands apart from Bow Fell itself. A narrow arête – with sweeping gullies on both side – connects the buttress with the main mountain. The most direct descent is to head south over exposed, broken ground to gain the scree shute that descends to easier ground and a circuitous path at the base of the crag.

Bow Fell's summit lies less than 200m to the west and is gained over rugged but easy-going ground. The views from here are superb and you can really appreciate what a magnificent piece of rock you have just climbed.

To the west lies Lakeland's highest and wildest tract of land and numerous and superb fell-walking routes abound. For a good and rugged trip, head south towards Three Tarns and then up on to the summit of Crinkle Crags (859m). Continue – all on well-trodden paths – on to Great Knott and then down to Oxendale and the main Langdale valley.

10. SCAFELL PINNACLE

DIRECT FROM LORD'S RAKE TO HOPKINSON'S CAIRN; LOW MAN FROM HOPKINSON'S CAIRN; AND THE KNIFE-EDGE ARÊTE

Mountain: Scafell (964m).

Cliff: Scafell Pinnacle.

Location: GR: 206068.

Grade: Severe.

Height: 116 m.

Time: 5–6 hrs.

Parking: National Trust car park; GR: 183074.

Maps: OS Outdoor Leisure (1:25000) sheet 6; OS Landranger (1:50000) sheet 96 or 97; Harvey's Map (1:25000 or 1:40000) Western Lakeland.

Guidebook: F&RCC – Scafell, Wasdale & Eskdale.

Equipment: Either an 11mm or, preferably, a 2 x 9mm rope and a rack including a full range of placements and at least three full-length slings. In addition, take a length of spare tape to fix up an abseil anchor.

Accommodation: Wastwater YH; tel: (01946) 726222.

INTRODUCTION

Scafell Pinnacle is closely associated with the early rock-climbing fraternity and in particular with O.G. (Only Genuine) Jones. The climbs put up on the Pinnacle around the turn of the century were right at the cutting edge of the sport; and even today, there are precious few undemanding routes to be found on this amazing piece of rock.

That Scafell Pinnacle should attract this early attention isn't surprising; what is remarkable is that it should have inspired the early pioneers to put up routes that were so technically demanding when there was so much unclimbed, but easier, rock to be developed elsewhere. The answer probably lies in the sheer magnificence of the piece of rock. Although it may be of modest height, in proportion it has the same qualities as the Dru, Cerro Torre and even the awe-inspiring Trango Tower. High, lofty pinnacles have always drawn climbers and have been a generation's proving place – Scafell Pinnacle was probably the first of these.

Anybody setting out up Scafell Pinnacle needs to know what they are about – even with today's modern gear it's a serious place. The combination of routes described isn't the easiest line on the crag but it's the most straightforward and it tackles the front of the Pinnacle and takes in the two summits of Low and High Man.

SITUATION

Scafell Pinnacle is one of four distinct buttresses that make up Scafell Crag and support Scafell's summit. They dominate the massive mountain cirque of Hollow Stones, between Scafell Pike and Scafell. The Pinnacle is defined in the east by Steep Gill and to the west by Deep Gill and is separated from the main Scafell massif by Jordan Gap. The top of the Pinnacle lies some 350m to the north-west of the mountain's summit.

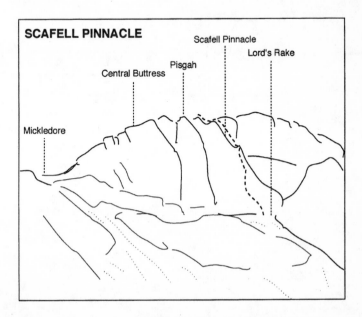

It's important to note that Mickledore, the col that lies to the east of Scafell, connects its summit with Scafell Pike and provides the usual climbers' descent from the crag, and has its own set of problems. The route from the summit plateau to the col is blocked by a notorious rock step called Broad Stand.

Broad Stand has been the site of quite a few accidents – mostly walkers trying to take the most direct route from Scafell Pike to Scafell. The scramble up it probably deserves a grade of about Very Difficult, and is deceptively exposed. It certainly requires the use of a rope.

APPROACH
The best approach is from Wasdale. From the National Trust car

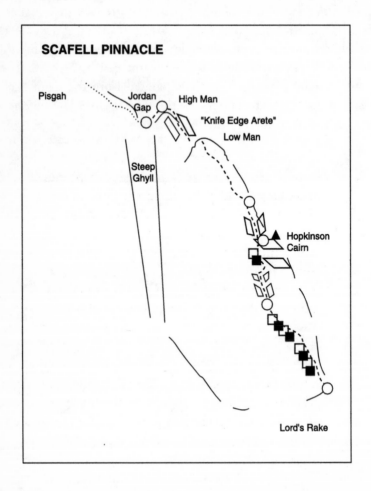

park, follow the signposted and well-trodden path up Lingmell Ghyll, Brown Cove and on to the large amphitheatre of Hollow Stones. Keep an eye out for a massive boulder – the Woolworth Boulder – and leave the main Mickledore track about 100m beyond it. A path now zigzags up to the base of the crag.

Scafell Pinnacle is approached by scrambling up to Pinnacle Terrace from the bottom of Lord's Rake. Go to the bottom right of the Pinnacle, above you will be able to see a leftwards-slanting rib that is reached by further scrambling. This is the common start of both Jones' Route Direct and Direct from Lord's Rake to Hopkinson's Cairn – the first section of our route.

1. Direct from Lord's Rake

CLIMB

Pitch 1:   A slabby ramp follows a rising traverse right to left. Gain the base of this up a delicate wall and follow the ramp for 12m to a grassy niche. The exposure is immediately apparent and you should concentrate on placing good running belays. It is important to remember that on any traverse these are equally important in protecting the second from a serious pendulum as they are for protecting a leader. Rig them with this in mind.

Pitch 2:   Here we part company with Jones' Route Direct as it continues off left. Seek out a corner on the right of the stance and climb this. It's topped off by a bulge which is climbed directly. This, in turn, gives way to another, steeper corner. Get in some good protection as this is followed by some dubious spikes-cum-flakes. A bold step up and to the right leads to a good ledge and a belay.

Pitch 3:   Next follows the crux of the route – Hereford's Slab. This is both steep, delicate and exposed. Rigging protection is problematic, but you should be able to get some small 'Rocks' in. Climb the slab to the left, then on and up to a ledge complete with a cairn – Hopkinson's Cairn. This is the end of the first climb.

2. Low Man from Hopkinson's Cairn

CLIMB

Pitch 1: You will now be high up on the front of the pinnacle. A number of climbs lead up from this point; this is the most straightforward and is graded as Difficult. Start from the left-hand edge of the ledge to gain a corner. Climb this directly. When you emerge, step right and go on to the front of the arête to a good belay.

Pitch 2: Climb straight up to a ledge and then move left to gain a wall, climb up this for two metres before you have to take an awkward step left to gain a grassy ledge. Belay here.

Pitch 3: Look left to a rising traverse along and up an obvious gangway, climb this directly up to easier ground and then there is a scramble to the top of Low Man.

3. Knife-edge Arête

CLIMB/SCRAMBLE

Pitch 1: Above – connecting Low Man with High Man – is the famous Knife-edge Arête. This is probably the best high-grade scramble in the Lake District; the only problem – from a scrambler's point of view – is that you need to be a rock-climber to get at it. Everything about it is superb and the exposure is incredible. It's given a moderate grade. The best approach is to climb it *à cheval* – which is French for 'on horseback'. You now arrive on the top of Scafell Pinnacle.

DESCENT

The descent is challenging at several stages; the first problem is getting off the top of the Pinnacle and into Jordan Gap. This involves a short climb down at a grade of about Difficult, or you can abseil; hence the recommendation to bring some spare tape – but don't use it all here.

From Jordan Gap a leftwards traverse avoids another graded

(Difficult) climb out of the gap and provides access to Scafell's summit plateau. Head north-east from the summit and off the plateau to pick up the Broad Stand path. It will eventually come to an end on a rock step above Broad Stand. This is only a 15m climb, but should be treated with caution as the drop on the Eskdale side is considerable.

An abseil is probably the best option. A short length of knotted tape will provide a good anchor from which the rope is more easily recovered than just by putting it around a spike. The ground remains rugged but it's scrambling rather than exposed climbing. Make your way along the ridge that forms the col and pick up the main path down into Hollow Stones.

11. GROOVED ARÊTE

Mountain: Scafell Pike (977m).

Cliff: Pike's Crag.

Location: GR: 209071.

Grade: Very Difficult.

Height: 125m.

Time: 5–6 hrs.

Parking: National Trust car park; GR:
181074.

Maps: OS Outdoor Leisure (1:25000)
sheet 6; OS 1:50000 Landranger
sheets 96 or 97; Harvey's Map

(1:25000 or 1:40000) Western
Lakeland.

Guidebook: F&RCC – Scafell, Wasdale &
Eskdale.

Equipment: Either an 11mm or,
preferably, a 2 x 9mm rope and a rack
including a full range of placements
and at least three full-length slings.

Accommodation: Wastwater YH; tel:
(01946) 726222.

INTRODUCTION

The Scafell massif is, without doubt, the most adventurous climbing range in the Lake District and is crowned by the highest summit in England, Scafell Pike. As befits its status, it's a high, wild place and feels very remote. Its supporting cliffs are uniformly magnificent and are home to some of the best climbing in the country.

Pike's Crag lies directly below the summit of Scafell Pike, so any climb up it leads directly to the highest point in England. Grooved Arête follows a direct but logical line, taking in the full height of the cliff and finishing at its highest point. It can be both technical and strenuous for its grade and the final pitch has a grand sense of exposure.

SITUATION

Pike's Crag forms the northern wing of the high-mountain cirque – known as Hollow Stones – that form the western ramparts of both Scafell Pike and Scafell. The girdling cliffs are split in two by the high-mountain pass of Mickledore. To the north lies Lingmell, to the south Mickledore Buttress and then the high, rocky col of Mickledore itself. Beyond the col, the cliffs swing round to due west to form Scafell Crag.

The most prominent feature on the Pike's Crag is Pulpit Rock; a massive arête that rears directly up from the floor of Hollow Stones to the crag's high point. Grooved Arête follows a commanding line up this.

APPROACH

See *10 Scafell Pinnacle.* Around 500m short of the col of Mickledore you will pass a large boulder – the Woolworth Boulder. About 100m after this massive rock, a subsidiary path branches off left from the main track. It can be followed over steepening ground to the path that girdles the base of Pike's Crag. Go to the lowest point of the cliff; this is the base of Pulpit Rock.

From the base of Pulpit Rock a prominent rib rises up, look to the right of this and you should be able to see a chimney capped by a large overhang.

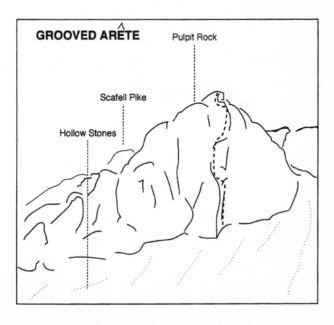

CLIMB

Pitch 1: The first pitch is over very broken rock and is more of a scramble than a climb; nevertheless rope up and place protection. Climb the rib and aim for a niche in the chimney below the overhang. Belay here.

Pitch 2: Things now start to get more exciting. Continue up the chimney until you can reach a thin traverse on the left-hand wall. The gully falls away steeply, and while there

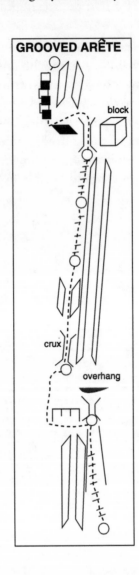

GROOVED ARÊTE

is good potential for protection, the rock is steep and the holds are small. The trick is not to go too high up the wall but to traverse left and use the line of the incut foot-holds. Handholds are also in short supply, and you feel out on a limb until a large sideways pull for a handhold appears and you can swarm round the corner and on to the front of the arête; larger and more comforting holds are to be found here. Continue on these up the front of the arête until you can gain a ledge. Belay here.

Pitch 3: Above is a chimney with comforting cracks for protection. Climb this to another ledge. Belay here.

Pitch 4: Now for the crux. You are faced with an off-width corner that, at first glance, looks straightforward but, in reality, can prove problematic. Start off by getting some protection in. Climb the crack until footholds run out and you are forced into a lay-back. Climb it in one go, and after three metres you can take the strain off your arms by bridging. Things will still feel insecure. Nevertheless you can get a no. 2 or a no. 3 'Friend' – or other active camming device – into a crack. It's worth having this to hand before you start. Continue on upwards, the holds now get better, until you reach a ledge.

Pitches 5 and 6: You now gain the main crest of the arête and this is followed over easier ground, though you should take care with some loose blocks. After two run-outs, belay below a massive block.

Pitch 7: To the right of the block, and separating it from the main ridge, is a chimney. Climb this to gain a ledge on the main ridge. The ledge now leads back round to the front of the arête. The footholds are large but the handholds aren't that abundant – particularly where there's a slight bulge to negotiate. Traverse along the ledge and then around the corner to the front of the arête. A series of exposed but straightforward slabs lead on to the top.

DESCENT

You are now atop an exposed pinnacle which is separated from the main mountain by gullies on the left and right and a steep notch between the rock and the hillside. The rope should be kept on. The quickest descent is to be found off to the right where you can scramble down over an exposed rockstep into a gully. It's filled with the usual scree and leads back to Hollow Stones.

Another option is to take in the summit of Scafell Pike; this lies less than 600m to the east. Once the notch across the connecting arête has been negotiated, easy scrambling leads to the summit plateau and the top of Scafell Pike.

From here there are a number of options for good walks; including a great mountain circuit that can be completed by dropping down north-west to Lingmell and picking up the Corridor Route to Styhead and then down to Wasdale Head.

12. NEEDLE RIDGE

Mountain: Great Gable (899m).	sheet 96; Harvey's Map (1:25000 or
Cliff: Napes.	1:40000) Southern Lakeland.
Location: GR: 210099.	Guidebook: F& RCC – Gable and Pillar.
Grade: Very Difficult.	Equipment: Either 11mm or 2 x 9mm
Height: 110m.	ropes; a rack including small to
Time: 5–6 hrs.	medium placements; at least three
Parking: Either Wasdale Head; GR:	full-length slings.
186087 or Seathwaite; GR: 235121.	Accommodation: Either Wastwater YH;
Maps: OS Outdoor Leisure (1:25000)	tel: (01946) 726222 or Borrowdale
sheet 6; OS Landranger (1:50000)	(Longthwaite) YH; tel: (01768) 777397.

INTRODUCTION

Most rock-climbers are aware of the significance of W.P. Haskett-Smith's first ascent of Napes Needle in 1886 which is usually considered to be the first rock-climb. Needle Ridge is named after this free-standing needle which is found at the base of the ridge – which was also climbed by Haskett-Smith, although this ascent pre-dates the first rock-climb by some two years. The first ascent of the ridge was seen as a way to reach Great Gable's summit – hence it falls well within the remit of a mountaineering rock-climb. It's a superb example of its type.

SITUATION

Great Gable's Napes Crag forms the upper reaches of the mountain's south-western flank. From this perspective it takes on its well-known pyramid form and is undoubtedly one of Lakeland's most handsome fells. The whole mountain stands isolated and aloof.

Napes consists of a series of sharp truncated arêtes, divided by

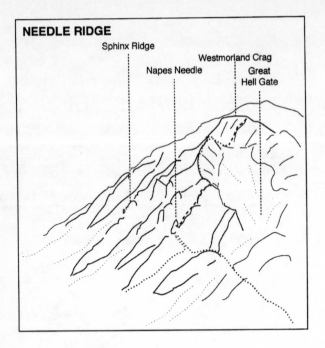

NEEDLE RIDGE

Sphinx Ridge

Westmorland Crag

Napes Needle

Great
Hell Gate

deep scree-filled gullies. Most of the routes on it have a mountaineering, rather than a technical climbing, feel. It's an impressive but welcoming place, with lots of good lower-grade routes.

The main section of the crag is defined by two large scree-filled gaps: Great Hell Gate to the right and Little Hell Gate to the left. Needle Ridge is the most easterly of the ridges, and its eastern side is flanked by the great rock wall of Tophet Buttress while to the west it is defined by Needle Gully. The rock is surprisingly continuous and of good quality. Climbing upon it is always good fun.

APPROACH

Great Gable stands in the west of the Lake District and to approach it from that side – from Wasdale – involves a long drive. The other option is to come in from the east via Borrowdale and Seathwaite. Both walks are of similar length and are along obvious paths. Both lead to the pass at Sty Head: GR: 219094.

From here, pick up the path that follows a rising traverse

between the Upper and Lower Kern Knotts and leads to Great Hell Gate. A subsidiary path branches off to the right and follows a higher line to, and beyond, Tophet Buttress. Walk below this until the Needle is reached. Gain the gap between the Needle and the main ridge; this can be done from either direction and is called 'Threading the Needle'. The climb rises directly above this.

CLIMB

Pitch 1: Above the gap behind the Needle rises a slab. This should be climbed directly to a stance below a groove.

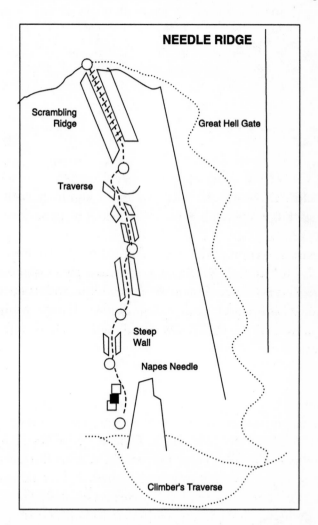

The rock is polished and can be slippery when damp. Protection can, however, be readily rigged; it should be done carefully as a slip could be serious. Gain a good stance below a steep wall and belay here.

Pitch 2: The wall is readily climbed via a groove and leads to another good ledge. Move right to gain the base of a rib and belay here.

Pitch 3: The rib is straightforward and leads to a belay stance below a corner.

Pitch 4: Climb the corner easily and then traverse left, below some overhangs, to gain an exposed and traversing ledge. Move along this, to the left and up, to gain the top of the climb. An exposed but straightforward scrambling ridge connects to a long neck of rock that, in turn, leads to the main mountain below Westmorland Crag.

DESCENT

The usual climbers' descent lies off to the left and down Great Hell Gate. The summit of Great Gable is but a short distance away. On this climb, in particular, the summit deserves to be included. It is easily reached by scrambling around and to the left of Westmorland Crag.

From Gable's fine rocky summit, your onward route will probably be dictated by where your transport is. For Wasdale Head, go back the way you came but continue down Little Hell Gate; for Borrowdale head down Gable's north-east ridge to Windy Gap and then cut down Aaron Slack to Styhead Tarn and the outward path.

13. ARROWHEAD RIDGE

Mountain: Great Gable (899m).
Cliff: Napes.
Location: GR: 209100.
Grade: Very Difficult.
Height: 80m.
Time: 5–6 hrs.
Parking: Either Wasdale Head: GR:
   186087; or Seathwaite: GR: 235121.
Maps: OS Outdoor Leisure (1:25000)
   sheet 6; OS Landranger (1:50000)
sheet 96; Harvey's Map (1:25000 or
   1:40000) Western Lakeland.
Guidebook: F&RCC – Gable and Pillar.
Equipment: Either 11mm or 2 x 9mm
   ropes; a rack including small to
   medium placements; at least three
   full-length slings.
Accommodation: Either Wastwater YH;
   tel: (01946) 726222 or Borrowdale
   (Longthwaite) YH; tel: (01768) 777397.

INTRODUCTION

Arrowhead Ridge is named after a prominent pinnacle that forms the truncated spur of the ridge. Although of the same grade as Needle Ridge, this route has a more serious air to it, due entirely to exposed ascent of the Arrowhead. It's well within its grade, however, and remains a fine way of climbing Great Gable.

SITUATION

Arrowhead Ridge is on the western side of Napes with only Sphinx Ridge remaining to its left. It's defined by Arrowhead Gully on the left and Eagle's Nest Gully on its right. Its main feature is the Arrowhead – a glacially truncated spur. This forms a steep wall, rather than a classic arête, in its lower reaches. Once this is cleared, the ridge levels out into a scrambling ridge.

APPROACH

See *12 Needle Ridge* to the Napes Needle. Then continue beyond the gully – Needle Gully – to gain a ledge, known as the Dress

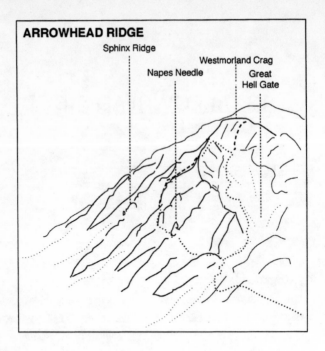

ARROWHEAD RIDGE

Sphinx Ridge

Westmorland Crag

Napes Needle

Great
Hell Gate

Circle. Follow the track – exposed in places – below Eagle's Nest Ridge, Abbey Buttress and across Eagle Nest Gully. The next prominent wall is the Arrowhead.

CLIMB

Pitch 1: Straightforward climbing up the front of the lower broken ridge gives way to steeper but more continuous rock and leads to a good ledge. Belay here.

Pitch 2: You are now approaching the Arrowhead and the crux of the climb. A chimney-cum-groove provides a way up this. Climb this directly. Above is an exposed slab, which is gained by a committing move – this should be well protected. Ascend the slabs directly, followed by a tricky move on to the point of the Arrowhead. Take a bold (and committing) step from the Arrowhead and on to a level ridge. Belay here.

Pitch 3: The technical climbing is now effectively over. The climb levels out and it is all scrambling from now on. It is exposed, however, so keep the rope on. Carry on until

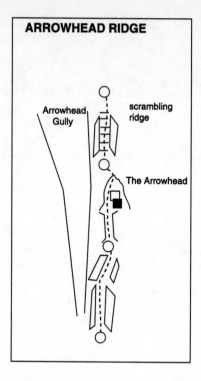

ARROWHEAD RIDGE

Arrowhead Gully

scrambling ridge

The Arrowhead

you reach the neck of rock that connects Napes to the main mountain and on to the rocks at the base of Westmorland Crag.

DESCENT
You can descend directly, either up and off to the left, then down by Little Hell Gate, or by going right, down Great Hell Gate. For the ascent of Great Gable and onward walks, see *12 Needle Ridge*.

14. SLEDGATE RIDGE

Mountain: Great Gable (899m).

Cliff: Gable Crag.

Location: GR: 213105.

Grade: Hard Severe.

Height: 73m.

Time: 4–6 hrs (including Oblique
  Chimney).

Parking: Honister Pass; GR: 225135.

Maps: OS Outdoor Leisure (1:25000)
  sheet 4; OS Landranger (1:50000)

sheet 89; Harvey's Map (1:25000 or
  1:40000) Western Lakeland.

Guidebook: F&RCC – Gable and Pillar.

Equipment: Either 11mm or 2 x 9mm
  ropes; a rack including small to
  medium placements; at least three
  full-length slings.

Accommodation: Honister Hause YH; tel:
  (01768) 777267.

INTRODUCTION

Gable Crag dominates Stone Cove on the northern side of Great Gable. It's an impressive, if broken, piece of rock that tops out just below Great Gable's summit. The routes on it tend to be much steeper and more serious than on the neighbouring Napes. While the rock is good, the cliff is broken up both vertically and horizontally and the climbs are not continuous.

Sledgate Ridge follows a relatively direct but broken line up the domed buttress on the crag's lower section. The climbing is exposed and technically satisfying. A logical continuation to the summit can be achieved by joining with Oblique Chimney – see *15 Oblique Chimney.*

SITUATION

Sledgate Ridge rises to two-thirds the height of Gable Crag before it's cut off by a pronounced ledge system. It's the most continuous piece of rock on the lower level. Above and to the right is Engineer's Slab, the dominant feature on the crag.

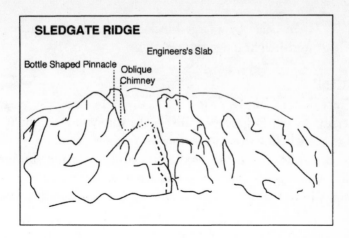

SLEDGATE RIDGE

Engineers's Slab

Bottle Shaped Pinnacle   Oblique
                          Chimney

APPROACH

The approach benefits from good accessibility. From the car park at the summit of Honistor Pass work your way through the abandoned quarry workings and on to the broad ridge that connects Grey Knotts, Brandreth and Green Gable. At Windy Gap pick up 'Moses Trod', the path that heads due west to the base of Gable Crag and then traverses around Great Gable.

Sledgate Ridge is found on the most continuous buttress on the lower section of the crag and rises directly from the scree. The climb starts up an obvious and steep crack on a short, steep wall. An easy chimney provides an option to the right.

CLIMB

Pitch 1: Climb the crack with difficulty, or the chimney with ease, before ascending the water-eroded crack. This leads to another chimney and then a good ledge. Move to the left of the ledge and belay here.

Pitch 2: The initial section of this pitch is up quite a fierce wall that then gives way to some exposed slabs. Head right and gain a large ledge. Belay here.

Pitch 3: Above is another steep wall broken in its upper reaches by a groove. Climb the groove but exit right to gain an obvious ledge. Above the ledge are three steep and exposed cracks. Climb the central one directly to the top then belay by a large block. You have now reached the mid-height ledge system.

DESCENT

A direct descent can be found off to the right along the ledge by traversing below Engineer's Slabs. Make sure you clear the top of a large gully below the slabs before you start descending.

To continue to the top of the crag and on to the summit of Great Gable, go left and then cut down to gain the base of a major chimney line. This is Oblique Chimney. See *15 Oblique Chimney*.

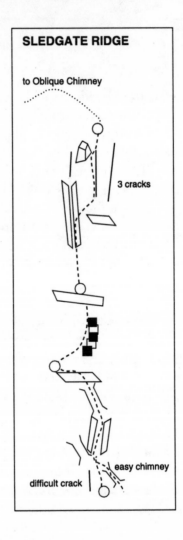

ABOVE: Comprehensive rack (clockwise from bottom left): climbing harness with self-rescue gear and 'Friends'; selection of slings; climbing rope; bandoleer with range of 'Rocks' and Hexcentrics

INSET: Boots (from top to bottom): general-purpose mountaineering boot; alpine rock boot; general-purpose sticky-soled climbing boot

Rucksack essentials (clockwise from bottom left): hat; headtorch; first-aid kit and emergency rations; penknife; bivvy mat and bivvy bag; thin gloves with grip pads; breathable jacket; helmet; fleece jacket; rucksack; camera; fluid sack; compass; map; guidebook and whistle; water bottle

Dow Crag
(Robin Ashcroft)

On the slabs of the second pitch of Giant's Crawl, Dow Crag
(Tony Shewell)

First pitch of 'C' Ordinary,
Dow Crag
(Robin Ashcroft)

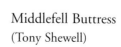

Middlefell Buttress
(Tony Shewell)

Pavey Ark
(Robin Ashcroft)

High up Pavey Ark
(Robin Ashcroft)

Negotiating the traverse on Grooved Arête, Pike's Crag
(Tony Shewell)

Moving clear of the big block and out on to the
final section of Grooved Arête, Pike's Crag
(Tony Shewell)

Pinnacle Rib's Yellow Slab
and the crack above it,
Tryfan's East Face
(Robin Ashcroft)

First pitch of Milestone
Direct, Milestone Buttress
(Robin Ashcroft)

Traditional antics on Tryfan's summit. Leaping
between Adam and Eve – not recommended when it's wet
(Robin Ashcroft)

High up Bristly Ridge's East Face
(Robin Ashcroft)
INSET: Bristly Ridge's East Face
(Robin Ashcroft)

Gribin Facet – the slabs are very obvious in the middle of the crag
(Robin Ashcroft)

Dinas Cromlech
(Robin Ashcroft)

15. OBLIQUE CHIMNEY

Mountain: Great Gable (899m).
Cliff: Gable Crag.
Location: GR: 213105.
Grade: Very Difficult.
Height: 23m.
Time: 4–6 hrs (including Sledgate
   Ridge).
Parking: Honister Pass; GR: 225135.
Maps: OS Outdoor Leisure (1:25000)
   sheet 4; OS Landranger (1:50000)
sheet 89; Harvey's Map (1:25000 or
   1:40000) Western Lakeland.
Guidebook: F&RCC – Gable and Pillar.
Equipment: Either 11mm or 2 x 9mm
   ropes; a rack including small to
   medium placements; at least three
   full-length slings.
Accommodation: Honister Hause YH; tel:
   (01768) 777267.

INTRODUCTION
Oblique Chimney is never going to be regarded as a classic Lake District climb. It does, however, provide a satisfying continuation to Sledgate Ridge at a reasonable grade and will put you at the top of Gable Crag, within a short distance of the summit of Great Gable.

SITUATION
Oblique Chimney is a pronounced feature on the upper section of Gable Crag. It's formed by a prominent pinnacle – called the Bottle-Shaped Pinnacle – and lies to the right and rear of this. As with many chimneys it can be a dark, occasionally dank, place. It rises directly from the mid-height ledge system.

APPROACH
From the top of Sledgate Ridge traverse left over broken ground until you reach the very obvious chimney by the Bottle-Shaped Pinnacle. Enter the chimney.

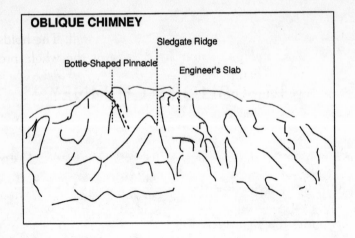

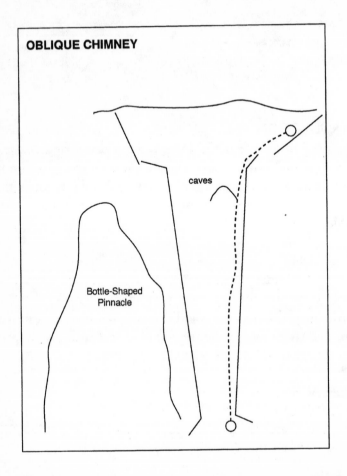

CLIMB

Pitch 1:   Climb the chimney using its right wall. The holds are good and protection apparent, but the whole process can be damp. At the top the way is blocked by two overhangs-cum-caves. Exit right and on to the top up a loose scree chute. Belay well back.

DESCENT

The descents aren't all that direct and involve going left or right for some distance to clear the crag and pick up Moses Trod. The top of Great Gable lies directly above; it is soon reached over broken ground which then gives way to the summit plateau.

From here, reasonably logical walking options are limited. The most practical is to descend Gable's north-east ridge and then pick up the outward path at Windy Gap.

16. GILLERCOMBE BUTTRESS

Mountain: Grey Knotts (697m).	sheet 4; OS Landranger (1:50000)
Cliff: Gillercombe Buttress (shown on	sheet 89; Harvey's Map (1:25000 or
some maps as Raven Crag).	1:40000) Western Lakeland.
Location: GR: 221124.	Guidebook: F&RCC – Borrowdale.
Grade: Severe.	Equipment: Either 11mm or 2 x 9mm
Height: 104 m.	ropes; a comprehensive rack; at least
Time: 4–6 hrs.	three full-length slings.
Parking: Seathwaite; GR: 235122.	Accommodation: Borrowdale (Long-
Maps: OS Outdoor Leisure (1:25000)	thwaite) YH; tel: (01768) 777257.

INTRODUCTION

Borrowdale, plunging deep into the central fastness of the Cumbrian Fells, is usually regarded as Lakeland's finest dale. Its cliffs, although superb, are seen as essentially valley crags. Gillercombe Buttress is the exception; it's a fine mountain cliff and its classic route is Gillercombe Buttress.

SITUATION

Grey Knotts towers over Borrowdale, splitting the valley between the main dale that leads on to Honister Pass and the smaller valley and settlement of Seathwaite. The fells above this small valley rise steeply; wooded on the lower slopes but ruggedly outcropped above.

Gillercombe buttresses the summit and forms its South-east Face. It's a somewhat broken, though large and quite impressive, cliff. The main section of the crag is defined on the left by Gillercombe Gully and on the right by an unnamed scree-filled gully. Below Gillercombe is Sourmilk Gill, a famous gorge and a well-known but tricky scramble.

APPROACH

A path leaves Seathwaite and follows an uncompromising line to the west of – and alongside – Sourmilk Gill. This leads into Gillercombe. As the path departs the gill, leave the path and follow the line of the stream into the hanging valley. Gillercombe looms above and is approached over marshy ground. To locate the climb, first locate Gillercombe Gully and then look right to the lowest rocks.

CLIMB

Pitch 1: This first pitch leads over slabs to a square recess; climb this to gain a ledge. Belay here.

Pitch 2: A series of ramps leads right, past some flakes, before cutting back right on a tricky traverse. A difficult move provides access to easier ground and a belay.

Pitch 3: A scrambling section leads to a large ledge at the foot of a groove. Belay here.

Pitch 4: Climb the groove, moving out on to the arête on the right, and then up to a belay stance.

Pitch 5: Climb into a steep corner and then go up this awkward section which, in turn, leads to another section of scrambling. Belay on a large ledge.

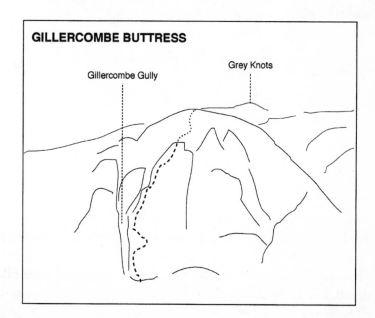

GILLERCOMBE BUTTRESS

Grey Knots

Gillercombe Gully

Pitch 6: Above is a groove and this is gained from atop a flake-cum-pinnacle. The groove is awkward and should be well protected. Exit this to reach some easier slabs, and climb to a belay stance at the foot of a groove.

Pitch 7: Ignore the groove and trend right on to some slabs. It is then easy climbing to the top.

DESCENT:

The usual climbers' descent lies off to the right and down a scree-filled gully. Grey Knotts' summit lies some 400m just to the north of east. Some good walking is to be found by heading south over Brandreth and Green Gable and descending Aaron Slack before returning via Styhead Gill.

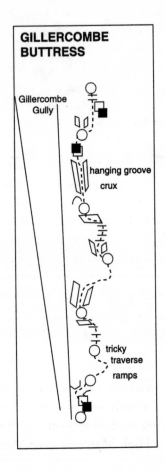

GILLERCOMBE BUTTRESS

Gillercombe Gully

hanging groove

crux

tricky traverse

ramps

17. NORTH-EAST CLIMB

Mountain: Pillar (892m).

Cliff: Pillar Rock – North-east Face.

Location: GR: 172123.

Grade: Mild Severe.

Height: 126m.

Time: 8hrs–2 days.

Parking: Ennerdale; GR: 109153; Buttermere; GR: 194150; Wasdale Head;
GR: 186087; Honister Pass; GR:
225135.

Maps: OS Outdoor Leisure (1:25000)
sheet 4; OS Landranger (1:50000)
sheet 89; Harvey's Map (1:25000 or
1:40000) Western Lakeland.

Guidebook: F&RCC – Gable & Pillar.

Equipment: 2 x 9mm ropes; a very
comprehensive rack; at least three full-
length slings; a length of tape for
abseil anchors.

Accommodation: Black Sail YH; GR:
195123; tel: via Alston YH (01434)
381509.

INTRODUCTION

Pillar Rock is one of the most impressive cliffs in Lakeland. As the name suggests, it's an isolated, conical crag that stands proud from its supporting fell. The three outward sides all present a steep prospect, while even the fourth – the uphill side – has a considerable, and steep, drop. It contains many excellent mountaineering climbs, many of which summit on the isolated pinnacle.

North-east Climb is found on the North-east Face of Pillar Rock. It follows a fine line that doesn't quite reach the summit but has some great situations nonetheless. There's a real feeling that you are on a considerable climb on a major cliff.

SITUATION

Pillar Rock extends from the northern flank of Pillar. The main structure of the rock trends north–south and in reality it's two cones of rock which are stacked one on top of the other with two individual summits – High Man and Low Man.

103

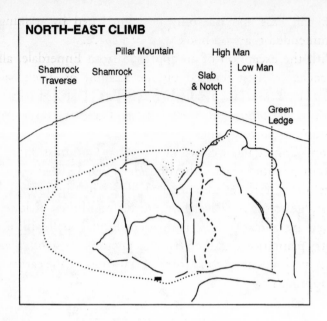

The northerly, eastern and western flanks are all of continuous steep rock of considerable height. The southern flank, which connects with the main mountain, is formed by the Jordan Gap, whose side, while not as high as the other flanks, is certainly as steep. To reach the summits of Low and High Man you will need to use handholds – even by the easiest route.

North-east Climb follows a fairly direct line that makes the best use of the cliff's features. The climb falls short of the summit of High Man but can be entertainingly, if tenuously, connected by using Slab and Notch – the easiest route to the summit and considered a classic scramble.

APPROACH

Pillar Rock is the most isolated crag in the Lake District and the closest parking is typically two hours away. In addition, the most direct approaches start from the western dales and this can involve a major drive around to the parking areas.

One convenient option is to base yourself for a few days at Black Sail Youth Hostel. This is a remote mountain hut close by

Black Sail Pass and can only be approached by walking. It is recommended that you book your bed space.

With the exception of an approach from Ennerdale, all other approachs are best focused on the summit of Black Sail Pass: GR:192113; and then follow the High Level Traverse – an advantage of coming this way is that you get a good view of Pillar Rock and its surroundings.

From Ennerdale, follow the Forestry Commission road (no entry to private vehicles) beyond the High Gillerthwaite Youth Hostel to a fork in the road. Follow the right fork, over a footbridge across the River Liza, turn left and then pick up a path marked by a cairn. This path ascends diagonally through the forestry plantation and then rises steeply to the base of Pillar Rock. Mountain bikes are a good form of transport in the early stages of this approach.

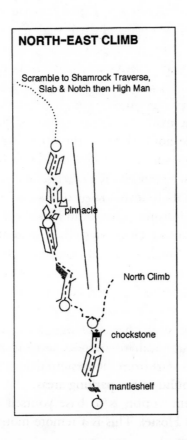

NORTH-EAST CLIMB

Scramble to Shamrock Traverse, Slab & Notch then High Man

pinnacle

North Climb

chockstone

mantleshelf

A rugged path that sits atop Green Ledge and leads to the Waterfall Crossing, skirts the base of Pillar Rock and provides access to all climbs. North-east Climb is found on the North-east Face on the left-hand side of Green Ledge.

CLIMB

Pitch 1: North-east Climb shares a common start with North Climb by way of a mantleshelf on to a prominent ledge above the start of Green Ledge. Move left and then up into a series of grooves and chimneys. Clear a chockstone on the left and then go right to clear the chimney and place a good belay.

Pitch 2: Head left, traversing some ribs and small slabs, to gain a belay at the base of a chimney. Belay here.

Pitch 3: Climb a series of chimneys – there are some awkward moves at the top – and then traverse left into a groove. Climb the groove and then belay in a recess.

Pitch 4: Cut right up into a corner and on to a pinnacle, then continue up a series of corners – one quite steep and awkward – to the top. Rough ground and scrambling to your left takes you to a path known as the Shamrock Traverse.

DESCENT

To use the Shamrock Traverse as a descent route turn east. To take in the summit of High Man, go north-west to reach Jordan Gap and the gully that drops down to the east – East Jordan Gully. From the foot of the gully go right for five metres, climb a step and then traverse the base of a slab and move on to the right. You will be able to gain a notch above and to the right. Climb up to and into this. This is the Slab and Notch.

When you exit, keep going right and climb a short rib. Then continue right across another slab overlooking an exposed gully. Then go right again and into a chimney and climb this before exiting left to the summit. It's all straightforward but well polished and very exposed. Keep your rope on.

To descend from the top of High Man you will need to reverse Slab and Notch; climbing down is always more tricky than coming up. While it isn't practical to abseil this because of the amount of traversing, it can be useful to use the rope as a handrail for short sections. The advantage of using 2 x 9mm ropes and having some spare tape for abseil anchors is now apparent.

Once you are back on the Shamrock Traverse it's all walking country and the summit of Pillar (Mountain, as opposed to Pillar Rock) lies some 200m to the south south-east over rough ground. From here the walking options are numerous and will depend on where you set out from.

18. WEST WALL CLIMB

Mountain: Pillar (892m).

Cliff: Pillar Rock – West Face of Low Man.

Location: GR: 171125.

Grade: Very Difficult.

Height: 76m.

Time: 8hrs–2 days.

Parking: Ennerdale; GR: 109153; Buttermere; GR: 194150; Wasdale Head; GR: 186087; Honister Pass; GR: 225135.

Maps: OS Outdoor Leisure (1:25000) sheet 4; OS Landranger (1:50000) sheet 89; Harvey's Map (1:25000 or 1:40000) Western Lakeland.

Guidebook: F&RCC – Gable and Pillar.

Equipment: 2 x 9mm ropes; a comprehensive rack; at least three full-length slings; and a length of tape for abseil anchors.

Accommodation: Black Sail YH; GR: 195123; tel: via Alston YH (01434) 381509.

INTRODUCTION

Unlike the climbs on Pillar's eastern flank, those to the west – on both the Low Man and High Man – go directly to the respective summits. Both the climbs and the summits are spectacular and superb situations can be enjoyed on their higher reaches.

West Wall Climb ascends the summit of Low Man, and High Man can then be reached by a straightforward scramble. As a climb it follows an almost perpendicular line but makes best use of the cliff's features. It's rightly regarded as a Lakeland classic.

SITUATION

Pillar Rock's western flank is divided into two walls the West Face of Low Man and the West Face of High Man – both supporting their respective summits. They are divided by the rising traverse of Old West Route, which forms a useful descent. West Wall rises from a large scree-filled gully and watercourse, called the

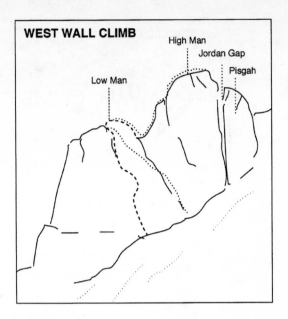

WEST WALL CLIMB

High Man

Jordan Gap

Pisgah

Low Man

Waterfall, and follows a line just below and to the left of the Old West Route; the two merge at the final few feet below the summit.

APPROACH

Follow the same general approach as *17 North-east Climb* and use Green Ledge to traverse around and into the upper reaches of the Waterfall. Old West Route provides a good reference point, as does the large boulder which you will see to the left of this. On the right is a ledge above a small wall; this is the start of the climb.

CLIMB

Pitch 1: Gain access to the ledge by a simple mantleshelf and then climb on to a second, larger ledge. A groove rises on the left-hand side of this and should be climbed directly – look to your protection – to an obvious pinnacle. Belay here.

Pitch 2: Traverse right and then climb to a rock bay, go past this to a crack and climb directly to a secure belay. Take care with your protection on the traverse and the crack as the rope can drag.

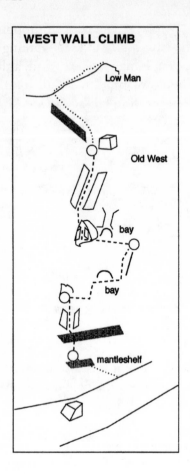

WEST WALL CLIMB

Low Man

Old West

bay

bay

mantleshelf

Pitch 3:   Traverse back right – below another bay formed by a
           chimney – to a collection of large rocks. Possible belay
           here. Above is a groove that is reached from a perch atop
           the rocks. Gain the groove – this can be awkward – and
           climb directly up it to Old West Route. Belay by a large
           boulder. From there, easy – though exposed –
           scrambling leads to the summit of Low Man.

DESCENT

A direct descent can be found down Old West Route but it is
exposed and the rope should be kept to hand.

A mountaineering option is to continue up the upper part of
the Old West Route and on to the broad arête that connects Low

Man with High Man. This is followed by dropping down into the col between the two summits and then working your way up the ridge. It goes at a scrambling grade of 3 and, although technically straightforward, should be protected with running belays as it is exposed. For the descent from High Man see *17 North-east Climb*.

19. NEW WEST CLIMB

Mountain: Pillar (892m).

Cliff: Pillar Rock – West Face of High
 Man.

Location: GR: 171124.

Grade: Very Difficult.

Height: 100m.

Time: 8hrs–2 days.

Parking: Ennerdale; GR: 109153;
 Buttermere; GR: 194150; Wasdale
 Head; GR: 186087; Honister Pass;
 GR: 225135.

Maps: OS Outdoor Leisure (1:25000)

sheet 4; OS Landranger (1:50000)
 sheet 89; Harvey's Map (1:25000 or
 1:40000) Western Lakeland.

Guidebook: F&RCC – Gable and Pillar.

Equipment: 2 x 9mm ropes; a comprehensive rack; at least three full-length
 slings; a length of tape for abseil
 anchors.

Accommodation: Black Sail YH; GR:
 195123; tel: via Alston YH (01434)
 381509.

INTRODUCTION

New West Climb follows an almost plumb-vertical line directly to the top of Pillar Rock's ultimate summit, High Man. It goes up some amazingly magnificent rock – its main mystery is that it can do this at such a modest grade. 'Classic' is an often misused word but not with regard to Pillar, and certainly not with this route.

SITUATION

The western flank of Pillar Rock is divided into two walls: the West Face of Low Man and the West Face of High Man – both supporting their respective summits. They are divided by the rising traverse of Old West Route, which forms a useful descent.

New West Climb rises direct to summit just to the left of west Jordan Gully from the Waterfall.

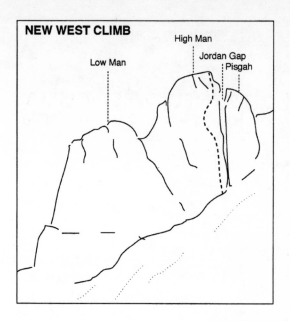

NEW WEST CLIMB

Low Man

High Man

Jordan Gap

Pisgah

APPROACH

Follow the same general approach as *17 North-east Climb* and use Green Ledge to traverse around into the upper reaches of the Waterfall. Go beyond Old West Route and find a large boulder just to the left of the bottom of Jordan Gully.

CLIMB

Pitch 1: Climb easily over the rocks and into a crooked groove. Emerge from this and move left to the base of a rib. Look right of this to a chimney and climb this to a pinnacle. Belay here.

Pitch 2: Traverse left to the base of a chimney and belay here.

Pitch 3: Above you rises a chimney and the crux pitch. How easy it is depends on your style – which may be inhibited given the considerable exposure; it is, however, readily protected. Some bridge it confidently, others thrutch it – the choice is yours. The former is the more stylish and less exhausting. At mid-height the chimney is blocked by a chockstone; so exit right, out on to the arête, before you get too intimately involved with it. Don't try to

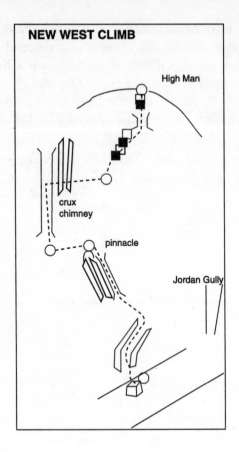

climb the arête but traverse right to a good belay by some perched boulders.

Pitch 4: Follow a rising traverse up some good slabs. The exposure will probably now begin to tell but the going is straightforward and the situation should be enjoyed. A short chimney leads to some more slabs and the summit. This is spectacular, whatever your criteria.

DESCENT

There are two options, both demanding. The first is to climb down Old West Route and this involves reversing the ridge between High Man and Old Man then going down the traversing ledge. This should be protected with a rope and it will return you to the Waterfall.

The other is to reverse the Slab and Notch. Find the gully that dissects the east side of the summit and descend this. Traverse right (direction given as if looking out) to a rib. Climb down this to a ledge, go right to a steep corner – Notch. Climb down this to a slab and traverse right, using the slab's lower edge. This leads to easier ground, Jordan Gap and the Shamrock Traverse. Given the traversing moves, a complete and straightforward abseil isn't an option but the spare tape is useful for providing an anchor for a short section to be descended. For walking options see *17 Northeast Climb.*

20. RIB AND SLAB CLIMB

Mountain: Pillar (892m).

Cliff: Pillar Rock – West Face of High Man.

Location: GR: 171124.

Grade: Severe.

Height: 100m.

Time: 8hrs–2 days.

Parking: Ennerdale; GR: 109153; Buttermere; GR: 194150; Wasdale Head; GR: 186087; Honister Pass; GR: 225135.

Maps: OS Outdoor Leisure (1:25000) sheet 4; OS Landranger (1:50000) sheet 89; Harvey's Map (1:25000 or 1:40000) Western Lakeland.

Guidebook: F&RCC – Gable and Pillar.

Equipment: 2 x 9mm ropes; a comprehensive rack; at least three full-length slings; a length of tape for abseil anchors.

Accommodation: Black Sail YH; GR: 195123; tel: via Alston YH (01434) 381509.

INTRODUCTION

Rib and Slab Climb crosses the same ground and shares some features with New West Climb but if you are capable of climbing at a higher grade then this will take you on an even more direct route. Having said that, it's well within its grade and again – an indication of the quality of climbing on Pillar – deserves its description as 'classic'.

SITUATION

Pillar Rock's western flank is divided into two walls: the West Face of Low Man and the West Face of High Man – both supporting their respective summits. They are divided by the rising traverse of Old West Route, which forms a useful descent. The Rib and Slab Climb rises between New West Climb and Old West Route.

116

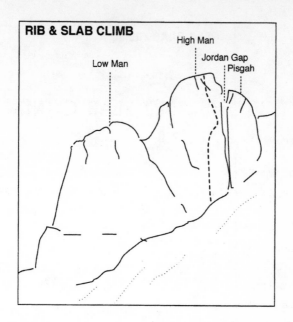

RIB & SLAB CLIMB

Low Man

High Man

Jordan Gap
Pisgah

APPROACH

See *17 North-east Climb*. Use Green Ledge to traverse round into the upper reaches of the Waterfall. Go beyond Old West Route and find a large boulder just to the left of the bottom of Jordan Gully. Go left again to a white intrusion which marks the start of the climb.

CLIMB

Pitch 1: Climb the easy, short walls interspersed by ledges and trend left to a broad but steep arête. Go up this by utilising two small chimneys on its face. Emerge from the second chimney and step right, out to a ledge. Belay here.

Pitch 2: Above is a steep groove; the crux of the climb is getting into it. Look to your protection. Things soon get easier and you break out left – closing with New West Climb – to an arête. Rib and Slab follows the crest of the arête, New West lies in the chimney to the left. Atop the arête, you step left and use the same pinnacle belay as New West.

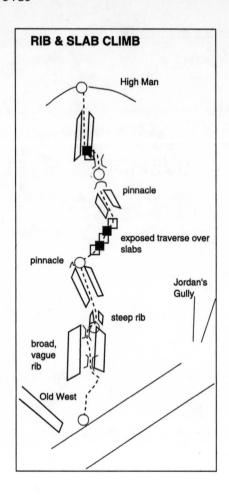

RIB & SLAB CLIMB

High Man

pinnacle

exposed traverse over slabs

pinnacle

Jordan's Gully

steep rib

broad, vague rib

Old West

Pitch 3: There now follows an exposed rising traverse over some slabs. The quality of the rock and the friction it provides is superb. The slabs merge with an arête and you should follow this to a second pinnacle belay.

Pitch 4: Again the route merges with New West and you climb a chimney before branching off to the left. Climb a straightforward slab and a final exposed arête to the top of High Man.

DESCENT

See *19 New West Climb.*

21. HARROW BUTTRESS, SLAB WEST ROUTE AND OXFORD AND CAMBRIDGE DIRECT

Mountain: High Stile (807m).

Cliff: Grey Crag.

Location: GR: 171148.

Grade: Severe.

Height: 100m.

Time: 5–6 hrs.

Parking: Buttermere; GR: 194150.

Maps: OS Outdoor Leisure (1:25000) sheet 4; OS Landranger (1:50000) sheet 89; Harvey's Map (1:25000 or 1:40000) Western Lakeland.

Guidebook: F&RCC – Buttermere and Eastern Fells.

Equipment: Either a single 11mm or 2 x 9mm ropes; a comprehensive rack; at least three full-length slings.

Accommodation: Buttermere YH; tel: (01768) 770245.

INTRODUCTION

Grey Crag is a remarkably friendly and accommodating place. It has many lower grade routes, good quality rock and is an ideal location for trying out mountaineering rock-climbing for the first time. The downside is that the climbing is broken but, by linking several climbs together, a pleasant expedition from combe floor to summit ridge can be made. This route suggests three diverse – in grade and character – climbs that nevertheless follow a reasonably direct and satisfying line.

SITUATION

High Stile rises directly above Buttermere and its dale and is part of a high ridge that thrusts out from the Cumbrian Fell's central core. The northern edge of this ridge is scalloped by a series of deep impressive hanging valleys – or combes – and the crags that enclose them are equally imposing.

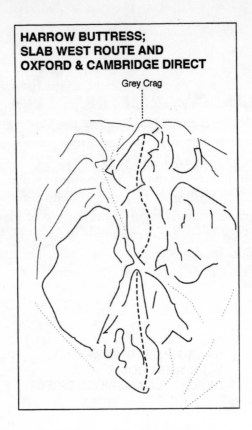

HARROW BUTTRESS;
SLAB WEST ROUTE AND
OXFORD & CAMBRIDGE DIRECT

Grey Crag

High Stile is a spur from the main ridge whose eastern flank is made up Grey Crag. It's riven into three layers by a number of transverse gullies and broad ledges. This route combines climbs on three distinct faces: the lower is Harrow Buttress; the middle is Grey Wall; the upper is Oxford and Cambridge Buttress.

APPROACH
High Stile and Grey Crag lie in the north-west quadrant of the Lake District, and the long drive to reach it is repaid by a very direct approach. Leave the road at Gatescarth and head south-west over the valley floor to clear the intake (the wall that marks the boundary between pasture and fell) and then follow a rising traverse on the right-hand branch of the path, until you reach Combe Beck. Follow this steeply into the combe; Grey Crag lies off to the west and is an obvious landmark. Go to the lowest point of the the crag.

1. Harrow Buttress

CLIMB

Pitch 1: This is a short first pitch: climb the arête to a good ledge. Belay here.

Pitch 2: Above the ledge leading left is a short chimney. Climb this and then go left again into a groove and then exit left to a good ledge. Belay here.

Pitch 3: Above and to the left is a broken groove, this is an easy climb that leads to a scramble up broken ground to a major transverse gully and the top of Harrow Buttress. Belay here. A short scramble down to the bottom of the next tier leads to Slab West Route. The next climb starts at a slab at the base of the buttress.

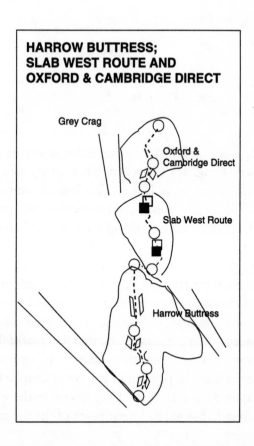

**HARROW BUTTRESS;
SLAB WEST ROUTE AND
OXFORD & CAMBRIDGE DIRECT**

Grey Crag

Oxford &
Cambridge Direct

Slab West Route

Harrow Buttress

2. Slab West Route

CLIMB
Pitch 1: The critical element to this route is delicate moves on slabs and the effective use of friction. Start up the slabs – you'll need to make best use of all possible protection – trending right and then left to a ledge below a bulge. Belay here.

Pitch 2: Climb left up a steep wall to a nose; negotiate this to the right and then continue straight on up until you can go left to reach a steepish slab and another large gully-cum-ledge. This is the top of Slab Route West. Belay here. Above is an arête that forms the crest of the upper buttress; Oxford and Cambridge Direct follows this.

3. Oxford and Cambridge Direct

CLIMB
Pitch 1: Climb the short but steep arête – first on the right and then on the left – before moving to its crest and then a ledge. Belay here.

Pitch 2: A crack leads off left; this is an awkward climb and quite steep. Climb it to a ledge on the right and continue over another bulge. Once over this, it is an easy route over rocks which leads to the summit ridge.

DESCENT
A direct descent to the bottom of the crag can be done by going either left or right and following the wide scree gullies to the base.

The summit of High Stile lies 100m to the north-west and provides access to some great walking. A good route to do takes in the summit then you should head south-east over High Crag and on to Scarth Gap Pass. An interesting descent takes you to the valley from here.

22. NORTH-WEST GROOVES

Mountain: Fairfield (873m).

Cliff: Hutaple Crag.

Location: GR: 367120.

Grade: Hard Severe.

Height: 114m.

Time: 5–7hrs.

Parking: Deepdale Bridge; GR: 399143.

Maps: OS Outdoor Leisure (1:25000) sheet 5; OS Landranger (1:50000) sheet 90; Harvey's Map (1:250000 or 1:40000) Centre Lakeland.

Guidebook: F&RCC – Buttermere and the Eastern Fells.

Equipment: Either an 11mm or 2 x 9mm rope and a rack including a full range of placements; and at least three full-length slings.

Accommodation: Patterdale YH; tel: (01768) 482394.

INTRODUCTION

While it's true that the Eastern Fells have fewer massive crags and good rock than those to the west, it is folly to dismiss them completely. Tucked away are the odd gems. It's also important to remember that the Helvellyn–Fairfield Range is the largest area of land over 2,000 feet in the area – and that it's been sculpted into a marvellous panorama. North-west Grooves is a great mountaineering challenge on good rock, amongst some of the most remote and sculpted scenery in the Lake District.

SITUATION

The whole of the eastern flank of the Helvellyn–Fairfield massif has been deeply sculpted by ancient glaciers. It's probably the most alpine-like scenery in the Lake District. Deepdale cuts deeper and further than most Lakeland dales and is very rugged.

At the head of the dale is a series of complex crags, of which Hutaple is the most continuous. It forms the northern flank of a

123

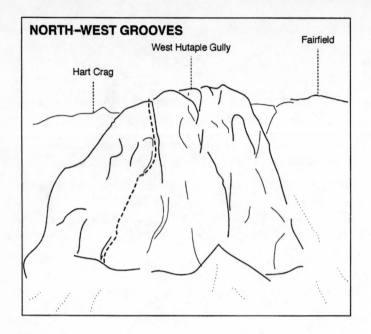

NORTH-WEST GROOVES

Hart Crag

West Hutaple Gully

Fairfield

major spur – Greenhow End – that projects into the upper dale dividing Link Cove from Gawk Cove.

APPROACH

A track leads from Deepdale Bridge deep into Deepdale; follow this beyond Wall End until it starts to peter out below Greenhow End. Climb the steepening hillside into Gawk Cove and then head south over scree to the base of the crag. Go to the lowest point of the rock.

CLIMB

Pitch 1: Identify a corner above the broken rock that forms the toe of the crag. Scramble over the rock to gain the corner. Climb the corner, either by its right wall or by the inner corner itself, to gain a ledge. Belay here.

Pitch 2: Easy rock leads to a ledge. Move right to another corner which is gained by way of an awkward mantleshelf. The corner is then followed to a large ledge below some overhangs. Belay here.

Pitch 3: Follow a line between the overhangs to gain a niche-

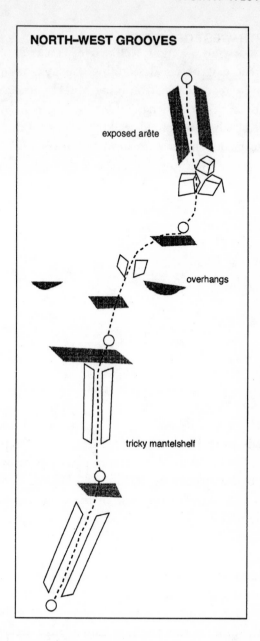

NORTH–WEST GROOVES

exposed arête

overhangs

tricky mantelshelf

cum-corner and then move right to a ledge. Belay by a flake.

Pitch 4: Traverse right and then climb some large blocks to gain an exposed arête. Follow this – there are good holds – to the top.

DESCENT

For a direct descent, go right, well above West Hutaple Gully, and then clear the crag before descending. Fairfield's summit is close by and can be reached by scrambling over the upper rocks of the Step and picking up the main ridge and then heading west on well-marked paths. Lots of fell-walking options abound from here, but the most convenient is to head back over Link Hause, Hart Crag, Hartsop above How and descend through Deepdale Park.

PART TWO

SNOWDONIA

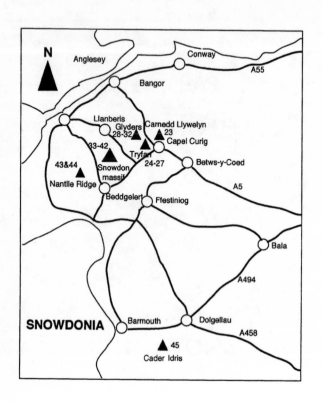

OVERVIEW

GEOGRAPHY

Snowdonia has 14 summits over 3,000 feet and its highest peaks are a good 300 feet higher than those of the Lake District. While it's generally accepted that the mountains of Snowdonia don't have quite the 'classic, romantic beauty' of the Lakeland Fells, it's readily acknowledged that they have a greater stature. There is no doubt that the extra height is manifested through more rocky and rugged summits. Many trips to the Welsh summits involve passages over steep and exposed rock. Mountain walking, scrambling and rock-climbing tend to merge readily into mountaineering.

The highest summit is Yr Wyddfa, usually referred to as Snowdon – although this latter, anglicised name also refers to the whole massif – at 1,085m (3,560 feet). All of the 3,000-feet-plus summits are found within the three most northerly ranges of the Carneddau, the Glyders and Snowdon. These run parallel to each other, trending from north-west to south-east. They are all separated by deep, rugged valleys. While these three massifs are counted as Snowdonia's major ranges, there are also other equally dramatic mountains to the south and east. Of particular note to the mountaineering rock-climber are the Moelwyns, the cliffs of Carnedd Silyn and the magnificent southern outlier of Cader Idris.

BACKGROUND

Like the Lake District, the first explorations on Welsh rock were viewed as a practice for alpine mountaineering and most of the early climbs – starting in the early 1880s – were done with a view to reaching a summit. Following on from the ascent of Napes Needle in the Lakes, rock-climbing as a separate sport developed rapidly in Snowdonia and produced the first of the senior climbing clubs – the Climbers' Club – in 1898 and the first 'pocket' guidebook, covering Lliwedd, in 1909. The Climbers'

Club continues to produce a comprehensive and definitive series of guidebooks that cover the area.

As with the Lakeland Fells, the Welsh mountains have had an influence on both climbing and mountaineering that far outweighs their modest altitude. Indeed, in the 1960s, the Welsh cliffs were probably one of the most important arenas for the development of rock-climbing techniques and skills anywhere in the world. For convenience the climbs in this book are listed around the main mountain ranges and follow a north–south progression.

APPROACHES
Although Snowdonia is distant from the motorway network, it's well served by major roads, some of which go directly through the mountain valleys. As a result, it's quite convenient to reach many of the major Welsh mountain groups and high cliffs by car. The northern ranges are best approached along either the A55 via Bangor or the A5 via Llangollen and Betws-y-Coed. To reach the mountains in central and southern Snowdonia, take either the A5 through Llangollen and then the A494 and head for Ffestiniog or Dolgellau, or the A458 through Welshpool and on to Dolgellau.

PUBLIC TRANSPORT
Snowdonia is poorly served by public transport. In the north, Betws-y-Coed can be reached by rail, but in the south the closest you can get is to Machynlleth. Onward bus connections into the valleys can be made – including the Sherpa Bus – but travel this way is time consuming.

CENTRES
Snowdonia, although a popular destination, isn't overly beset by the tourist industry. Betws-y-Coed and Llanberis are the only recognisable tourist traps. The other centres are Dolgellau, Ffestiniog, Beddgelert and Bethesda. There is, however, a good selection of youth hostels and campsites in the mountain valleys – Pen-y-Pass and Idwal Cottage having very strong mountaineering connections – along with one or two pubs which offer rooms. Of particular note is the Pen-Y-Gwryd Inn, complete with its collection of Everest memorabilia.

23. AMPHITHEATRE BUTTRESS

Mountain: Carnedd Llewelyn (1,062m).
Cliff: Craig yr Ysfa.
Location: GR: 694634.
Grade: Very Difficult.
Height: 300m.
Time; 5–7hrs.
Parking: Cwm Eigau car park; GR: 732663.
Maps: OS Outdoor Leisure (1:25000) sheet 16; OS Landranger (1:50000) sheet 115; Harvey's Map (1:25000 or 1:40000) Snowdonia North.
Guidebook: CC – Carneddau.
Equipment: Either a 11mm or 2 x 9mm rope; a rack including a full range of placements, at least three full-length slings.
Accommodation: Rowen YH; tel: (01492) 530627.

INTRODUCTION

Of all of Snowdonia's principal ranges there is no doubt that the Carneddau are the most remote. Any expedition into them is likely to be a lonely business. In form they tend towards massive bulk rather than the angular cragginess of their northern neighbours. They do, however, contain some very fine crags, mostly within the deep valleys that penetrate the range's central core. Few crags in the UK are as remote as Craig yr Ysfa.

Amphitheatre Buttress is a remarkably long, satisfyingly direct and sublimely remote route. Its challenge lies not in its technical difficulties but in its position. Having said that, its crux – up a well-worn corner – will try all but the most determined leader and thrill with its massive sense of exposure. After a brief respite comes a spectacular knife edge and set of pinnacles – marvellous mountaineering.

SITUATION

Craig yr Ysfa is found high on the eastern flanks of Carnedd

AMPHITHEATRE BUTTRESS

Amphitheatre Buttress

The Amphitheatre

Great Gully

Llewelyn, Snowdonia's second-highest summit, rising above the remote Cwm Eigau. Amphitheatre Buttress is named for – and defined by – the Amphitheatre, an enormous gully that lies to its right. To the left it's bounded by Avalanche Gully.

The Carneddau are renowned as receiving the worst weather in Snowdonia. The crag is also east facing, so it usually requires a few days of dry weather for this route to be in a decent condition.

APPROACH

Leave the car park and follow the track to an old dam below the reservoir. Cross the Afon Porth-Ilywydd and continue on up into Cwm Eigau, past some old buildings. Beyond these you turn into the main cwm and will be able to see the crag to the west. A path leaves the main track and leads to the scree below the ridge of Amphitheatre Buttress.

CLIMB

Pitch 1: Identify the Amphitheatre and look left to scramble up the rocks at the toe of the buttress and belay below some slabs. Climb the slabs and then climb a corner to belay a good stance.

Pitch 2: Climb a spiky rib to gain some more slabs and then gain a large ledge. Belay here.

Pitch 3: Above is the crux. Get into, and then climb, a corner before traversing left to gain a steep wall. Climb the crack behind the block and then scramble to a large ledge. Belay here.

Pitch 4: The next section is straightforward scrambling. Belay at the base of an arête.

Pitch 5: Traverse the airy and pinnacled, but technically straightforward, arête. Belay at the end of this.

Pitch 6: A good ridge leads to the summit plateau.

DESCENT

The most direct descent lies off to the left following Carnedd Llewelyn's south-east ridge to Bwlch Eryl Farchog; descend steeply from here.

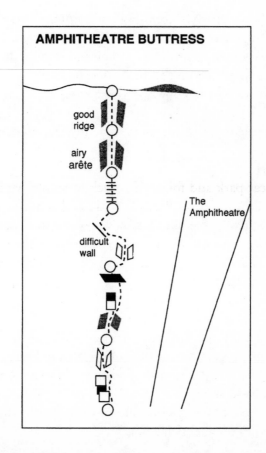

AMPHITHEATRE BUTTRESS

good ridge

airy arête

difficult wall

The Amphitheatre

Carnedd Llewelyn's summit lies 600m to the west and can be easily gained along the south-east ridge. From here head north to Foel Grach and then cut back down to Cwm Eigau and the outward path.

24. MILESTONE DIRECT

Mountain: Tryfan (915m).
Cliff: Milestone Buttress.
Location: GR: 663601.
Grade: Very difficult.
Height: 90m.
Time: 3–4hrs.
Parking: Lay-bys on A5; GR: 663603.
Maps: OS Outdoor Leisure (1:25000) sheet 17; OS Landranger (1:50000) sheet 115; Harvey's Maps (1:25000 and 1:40000) Snowdonia North.
Guidebook: CC – Ogwen
Equipment: 2 x 9mm ropes; a rack containing mostly small to medium placements; at least three full-length slings; and a length of abseil anchor tape.
Accommodation: Idwal Cottage (Ogwen) YH; tel: (01248) 600225.

INTRODUCTION

Milestone Direct is named after Milestone Buttress, which in turn is named after the old 'milestone' on the A5. This should define it as a roadside crag, perhaps? Of all our mountains, however, there are none which rise so distinctly – and abruptly – above the valley floor as Tryfan. The moment you leave the road, you are under no doubt you are on a mountain.

Milestone Buttress is Tryfan's major feature on its western flank and, although low down, is essential to the mountain's structure and can be included in a challenging mountaineering ascent of Tryfan. Milestone Direct, in turn, connects the main features on the crag to provide a remarkably direct and stimulating climb. It's always challenging – within its grade – and the rock architecture is magnificent. It is, however, best to get on it, and up it, before the crowds arrive.

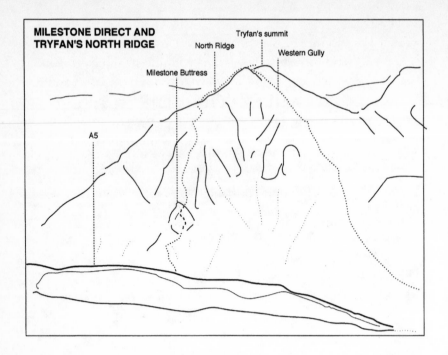

**MILESTONE DIRECT AND
TRYFAN'S NORTH RIDGE**

Tryfan's summit

North Ridge

Western Gully

Milestone Buttress

A5

SITUATION

Milestone Buttress is located on Tryfan's western flank well into the angle formed by the mountain's North Ridge. The crag has two facets: the slabs of the Front of the Milestone – the area we are interested in – and the Back of the Milestone. The front is obvious and open, while the back is tucked off to the left and is dark and complex.

Milestone Direct starts up a crack that bisects the fine slabs on the front of the buttress, just to the right of the crag's lowest point. The rock is clean – if a little polished – and sound.

APPROACH

Leave the road by the stile near the lay-bys and follow a well-trodden and graded path up by a wall. Cross the wall at the second stile and skirt up the scree to the lowest point of the rocks. Look slightly right to an obvious clean slab and identify a crack line. This is the start of Milestone Direct.

CLIMB

Pitch 1: Ascend the slab making best use of the crack; it does tend to flare so you will need quite small placements for protection. Don't be drawn too far up the crack and start looking towards the overhanging corner to the left. At a horizontal crack, traverse left towards the corners and use this to climb towards the pronounced pinnacle-cum-flake. A crack, above and to the right of the pinnacle, appears to be attractive – ignore it, it only makes life more difficult. Place some protection behind

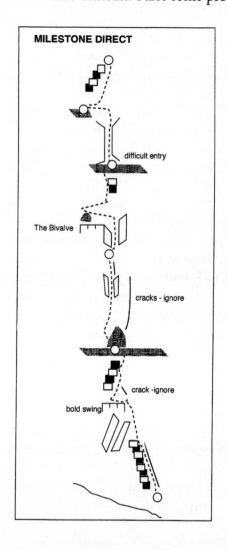

MILESTONE DIRECT

difficult entry

The Bivalve

cracks - ignore

crack -ignore

bold swing

the flake, curl your hands over the top of it and then commit yourself to the first hand traverse. The trick is to get your feet on the outside and take the weight off your hands. Once committed it's quite straightforward. After the traverse, gain some slabs that lead to a good belay ledge complete with a solid spike. Belay here.

Pitch 2: Behind the spike is a groove that narrows to a crack. Both are climbed directly and can be well protected – but take care, as you will tend to get your knee stuck if you get too far into the crack. At the top of the crack is a stance below another prominent pinnacle – known as the Bivalve. Belay here.

Pitch 3: A series of smaller spikes leads up to the Bivalve; climb these to gain a flake and a second hand traverse. As with the previous one, it is readily protected, and judicious use of your feet will take the strain from your arms. Cut back behind the pinnacle to a large ledge complete with a good thread belay.

Pitch 4: Up till now, each pitch has had its own crux, and the final one is no different. This time it's in the form of a chimney that is just too narrow to get into and too wide apart to jam. It's approached up some more slabs. Again it's readily protected, but it's awkward; a combination of arms, shoulder and knee seems to do the trick. Once you emerge from the top of the chimney the going is more straightforward but two-thirds of the pitch remains. A traverse along a ledge, another groove and then some slabs will see you to the top.

DESCENT

The direct descent is tricky and you should keep your rope to hand. Head right and cross the top of one gully to gain some slabs. Traverse these to gain a second gully which can be descended – although take care with some of the short but exposed steps.

To take in the summit, scramble up broken ground and rock to gain the North Ridge. This section is mostly scrambling with few well-defined options. You should be channelled on to the North Ridge near a prominent feature called the Cannon.

Tryfan's North Ridge is one of Snowdonia's classic ridge scrambles. The ridge is actually quite broad and the scrambling consists of serried ranks of short walls and then subsidiary summits before a rocky, isolated peak marks the top. A good descent is down Western Gully. This is reached by heading north and then west; the path is well scuffed and the gully channels you into the right route to descend through the upper crags.

Another option is to descend Tryfan's Southern Ridge to the col at Bwlch Tryfan and take in an ascent of Bristly Ridge and a descent of Gribin Ridge – it's a superb round.

25. GROOVED ARÊTE

Mountain: Tryfan (915m).

Cliff: East Face – North Buttress.

Location: GR: 666597.

Grade: Hard Very Difficult.

Height: 240m.

Time: 5–7hrs.

Parking: Glan Dena; GR: 668605.

Maps: OS Outdoor Leisure (1:25000) sheet 17; OS Landranger (1:50000) sheet 115; Harvey's Maps (1:25000 or 1:40000) Snowdonia North.

Guidebook: CC – Ogwen.

Equipment: Either an 11mm or 2 x 9mm rope; a rack including a full range of placements; at least three full-length slings.

Accommodation: Idwal Cottage (Ogwen) YH; tel: (01248) 600225.

INTRODUCTION

Grooved Arête is one of the best of Snowdonia's classic mountaineering rock-climbs – a great route in a superb situation. Although Tryfan's north peak is the lowest of its principal summits, it's a fine mountain nonetheless. Grooved Arête utilises its principal line and employs its most important features.

The route – despite its modest grade – is no pushover and it is a committing route with an exposed finish. As with all of Tryfan's climbs, the rock is sound, the holds always adequate and the protection readily available.

SITUATION

Tryfan's skyline is readily recognisable as you leave Capel Curig for the Ogwen Valley. Usually referred to as a 'shark's fin' of a mountain, it's an apt description. Although three sharks' fins may be even more correct.

Tryfan's north summit is the right-hand one of the three main towers – the three fins. It's supported on the right by the impressive North Ridge and defined on the left by Central Gully. It's the

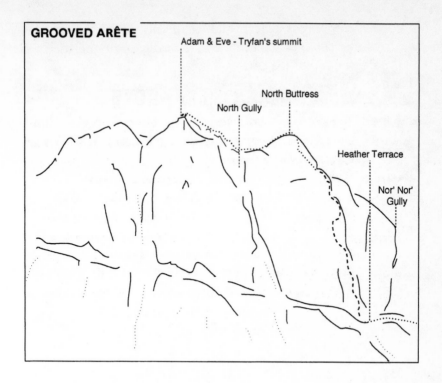

most continuous rock on the face. Grooved Arête follows the right-hand skyline to join the North Ridge below the summit.

APPROACH
Leave the A5 by the stile on the opposite side of the road to Glan Dena and follow the track south below Tryfan Bach. Hereabouts a path branches off west to cut up to the northern end of the Heather Terrace. Gain this and go below the rocks until you gain Nor' Nor' Gully. Grooved Arête starts just beyond this.

CLIMB
Pitch 1: Beyond Nor' Nor' Gully is a second, smaller gully, Green Gully. Grooved Arête starts at a rib six metres to the left of this. Look to a detached flake, climb the corner behind this. Exit the corner and trend left to a rib topped by a tall spike. Belay here.

Pitch 2: Go left for an exhilarating pitch up a corner. The

climbing is delicate and technically demanding but can be climbed smoothly and is readily protected. Belay at the top of the corner.

Pitch 3: Above is a steep step-cum-overhang, climb this directly to gain a ledge, trend right and belay below a rib.

Pitch 4: You are now about to gain the Grooved Arête. Climb the arête until you can go no further and are forced left into the groove. Belay here.

Pitch 5: Work up left to gain the groove and ascend this directly. The position is exposed and feels quite serious. Take care with your protection. Belay at a ledge below a slab.

Pitch 6: Towards the left-hand edge is a crack-cum-chimney that cuts up to the slabs. The crack is awkward but can be protected – it's a pure thrutch! Above is Knight's Slab. This is a compact and exposed slab – success depends on

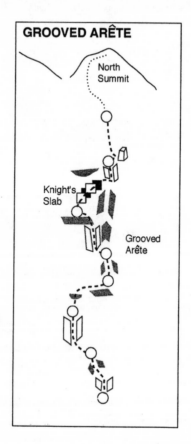

GROOVED ARÊTE

North
Summit

Knight's
Slab

Grooved
Arête

a series of delicate moves on small holds. Follow a rising traverse to the right to gain a niche round a corner. This leads to a comforting belay by a large block.

Pitch 7: A steep, but easy, wall leads up to the top of the climb and on to scrambling to the North Ridge, which leads to both the north summit and the central (main) summit.

DESCENT

A direct and sporting descent can be taken back down the North Ridge. You can, however, complete a full traverse of the mountain to Bwlch Tryfan – the col that divides Tryfan from the Glyders – where a number of options present themselves. The first is to head up Bristly Ridge and then descend down Gribin Ridge; the second is to head south over the col and follow the Heather Terrace back to the outward path and directly to the start point. This latter is a convenient and enjoyable option.

26. PINNACLE RIB
INCLUDING THOMSON'S CHIMNEY

Mountain: Tryfan (915m).
Cliff: East Face – Central Buttress.
Location: GR: 665594.
Grade: Mostly Difficult but with a short section at about Hard Severe.
Height: 175m.
Time: 4–5hrs.
Parking: Lay-by at Glan Dena; GR: 668603.
Maps: OS Outdoor Leisure (1:25000)
sheet 17; OS Landranger (1:50000)
sheet 115; Harvey's (1:25000 and 1:40000) Snowdonia North.
Guidebook: CC – Ogwen
Equipment: Either an 11m or 2 x 9mm ropes; a comprehensive rack with a good selection of small to medium placements.
Accommodation: Idwal Cottage (Ogwen) YH; tel: (01248) 600225.

INTRODUCTION

Tryfan's is undoubtedly one of the most impressive pieces of mountain architecture to be found in Snowdonia. Pinnacle Rib Route follows an entirely logical line up the mountain's magnificent East Face on its Central Buttress, emerging directly on to an isolated and angular summit. Interestingly, this route was the first of Tryfan's rock-climbs to quit the confines and psychological security of the gullies and move out on to open rock.

The climbing is – as is the norm on Tryfan's East Face – mostly very straightforward, with the exception of the notorious Yellow Slab. This requires both some delicate friction work and fluid, confident moves. It's a pitch to be avoided if it's wet, but can be protected and, if not practical, can be bypassed.

SITUATION

Central Buttress is the highest of Tryfan's famous cliffs and the one that supports the summit. It consists of sound, continuous rock between the Heather Terrace and the two 'gendarmes' – Adam and Eve – that form the summit. Bounded on both sides by well-defined gullies, it fulfils the childhood dream of what a mountain should look like.

APPROACH

See *25 Grooved Arête*, but continue beyond North Buttress and clear North Buttress and North Gully to gain the base of Central Buttress. Pass beyond a second smaller gully – called Little Gully – and then locate an obvious grass bay; Pinnacle Rib climbs the rib on the right of this.

CLIMB

Pitch 1:   The rib is split by a corner, climb this and then up the front of the rib. Possible belay at the top of the arête. Then trend to the right to gain the corner that is capped

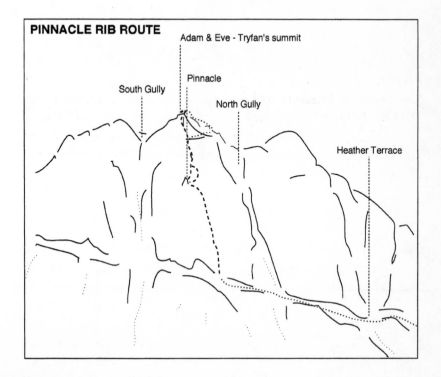

PINNACLE RIB ROUTE

Adam & Eve - Tryfan's summit

Pinnacle

South Gully

North Gully

Heather Terrace

by a bulge. This is split by a crack and can be climbed directly. Belay on the ledge atop this.

Pitch 2: The rib continues upward trending to the right – it is very broken and mostly consists of climbing a series of rock steps. These lead to a large terrace and the pinnacle. Belay here.

Pitch 3: Above and to the right is the Yellow Slab; this is the crux of the climb and a beautiful piece of wrinkled rock. It requires a combination of delicate moves and bold, fluid climbing. Climb the left-hand edge up a series of small footholds. You'll feel off balance, but you can get a number one or two Super Rock into a small crack. You'll probably feel the need to retreat once it's placed. From the steps on the edge of the slab move out on to the slab, relying on friction and a belief in yourself. Sanctuary in a widening crack beckons, but take care, as you'll lunge

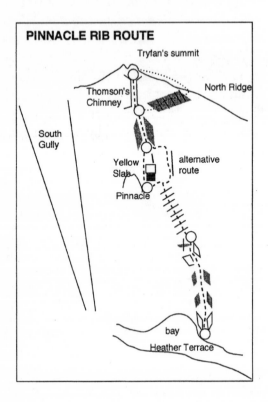

at your peril. Remain calm and concentrate on using your feet properly; respite will come in due course. Once you are in the crack, take a breather, get some protection in and then climb on. Belay at a ledge.

Pitch 3: Wet weather alternative. Yellow Slab needs to be dry to be climbed. An alternative pitch can be found up a crack around the corner to the right.

Pitch 4: The final pitch is superb; a seemingly broken rib – it looks like a Cadbury's Flake – curves in an exposed arc upwards. The rock is surprisingly sound and provides good, if simple, climbing to the top.

Thomson's Chimney

CLIMB

Pitch 1: Pinnacle Rib comes to an end on a large scree-covered ledge directly below Tryfan's summit. The easiest option is to traverse left and then right which takes you over easy ground to gain the North Ridge and then the summit. There is, however, a direct option – Thomson's Chimney. It is graded as Very Difficult and goes in one pitch – it is a thrutch and tends to be damp. Look to the back wall, the chimney is obvious. Just get yourself into it via a ledge on the left and go for it!

DESCENT
See *25 Grooved Arête.*

27. GASHED CRAG

Mountain: Tryfan (915m).

Cliff: East Face – South Buttress.

Location: GR: 665593.

Grade: Hard Very Difficult.

Height: 210m.

Time: 4–5hrs.

Parking: Lay-by at Glan Dena; GR: 668603.

Maps: OS Outdoor Leisure (1:25000)

sheet 17; OS Landranger (1:50000) sheet 115; Harvey's (1:25000 and 1:40000) Snowdonia North.

Guidebook: CC – Ogwen.

Equipment: 2 x 9mm ropes; a comprehensive rack and at least three full-length slings.

Accommodation: Idwal Cottage YH; tel: (01248) 600225.

INTRODUCTION

Gashed Crag is the third of Tryfan's great mountaineering rock-climbs, this time ascending to the Southern Summit. This is the most continuous of the routes and the quality of the climb is maintained throughout. It's named after the prominent 'V' gash seen on the skyline.

SITUATION

Gashed Crag is found on the South Buttress; it's a fine, isolated piece of rock. This route follows an obvious and well-defined line, up the right-hand edge of the face; defined on the right by South Gully and on the left by the remainder of the face. As with most of Tryfan's climbs, the rock is sound, the holds always there and protection to hand.

APPROACH

See *26 Pinnacle Rib*, but continue beyond Central Buttress and clear South Gully, then look for a steep rise in the path and a buttress with an overhang above.

CLIMB

Pitch 1: Look to the right-hand edge of the buttress which is split by a corner capped by an overhang. Climb the crack and clear the overhang to the right. Belay here.

Pitch 2: Trend to the left to gain a crack on the front of the groove, climb this difficult but direct route to the large ledge below and overhang. Belay here.

Pitch 3: Walk to the right-hand edge of the ledge to clear the overhangs – the Gash – and into a chimney. This is both smooth and tight and invariably becomes a struggle. Get up it to clear the overhangs and gain a stance. Belay here.

Pitches 4–7: Move right and then back left with a committing move to regain the main ridge. Follow this – it is mostly straightforward but it does have an awkward step to negotiate. It ends in a dark recess.

Pitch 8: Go right on to and into a deep corner that then leads to

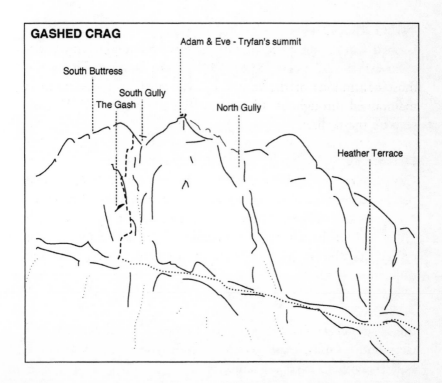

quite an awkward and narrow chimney – climb this. Scrambling then leads to the summit.

DESCENT

Tryfan's main summit lies to the right and is reached via the rocky but broad Southern Ridge. See *25 Grooved Arête*.

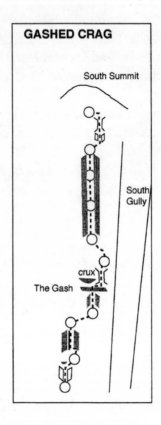

28. SLAB DIRECT AND SLAB ROUTE

Mountain: Glyder Fach (994m).

Cliff: Gribin Facet and Glyder Fach's Main Cliff.

Location: GR: 649596 and GR: 656585.

Grade: Very Difficult.

Height: 62m and 85m.

Time: 5–6hrs.

Parking: Ogwen Cottage; GR: 649603.

Maps: OS Outdoor Leisure (1:25000) sheet 17; OS Landranger (1:50000) sheet 115; Harvey's (1:25000 and 1:40000) Snowdonia North.

Guidebook: CC – Ogwen.

Equipment: 2 x 9mm ropes; a comprehensive rack; and at least three full-length slings.

Accommodation: Idwal Cottage (Ogwen) YH; tel: (01248) 600225.

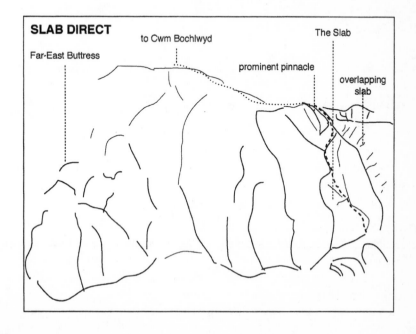

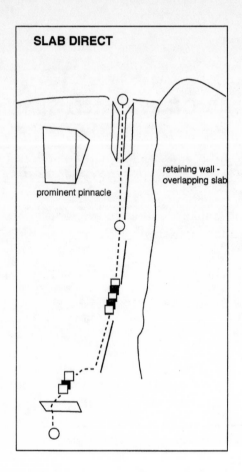

INTRODUCTION

Glyder Fach's main cliff commands a dominating position over the Ogwen Valley and Cwm Bochlwyd in particular. It buttresses Glyder Fach and lies just below the rocky summit plateau. A broken cliff, it nevertheless has some fine, classic routes, all of which are in a high-mountain environment.

Below the lip of Cwm Bochlwyd is the Gribin Facet, in many respects a valley crag but with some good long routes nonetheless. By combining both cliffs you can enjoy an expedition that spends a lot of its time on rock but ascends over 600m from valley floor to summit plateau.

On Gribin Facet the most direct route is Slab Direct. While

Glyder Fach has several classic mountaineering climbs – which you are likely to have all to yourself – Slab Route ties in most characteristics of the cliff.

SITUATION
Gribin Facet is the classic truncated spur, produced when a glacier sheared off the bottom end of Gribin Ridge. The slab is the dominant feature on the cliff and can be seen from some distance away.

Glyder Fach's main cliff is also the product of ice, this time the plucking action of the small glacier in Cwm Bochlwyd and later freeze-thaw shattering. It's a broken cliff that produces some good but non-continuous climbs. There's certainly no shortage of lines on the face. Slab Route is relatively continuous but utilises the cliff's weaknesses and leads directly to the summit plateau.

APPROACH
Leave Ogwen Cottage by Idwal Path, but leave it after 200m at a junction. A second path leads on towards Cwm Bochlwyd and this should be followed for a further 350m. Gribin Facet and the slabs will now be in view and, at a convenient point, you can leave the path and contour round to their base.

1. Slab Direct

CLIMB
Pitch 1: The line of Slab Direct, once on to the slab, is obvious, but gaining the slab isn't and the start of a neighbouring climb is used. Start at the bottom right-hand corner of the steep wall at the base of the slab; gain a large ledge and then trend right and above and on to the slab to gain a crack system. Simply follow this up using a combination of crack and slab climbing to gain a ledge halfway up. Belay here.

Pitch 2: Aim for the gap between the pinnacle to the left and the retaining wall to the right. The crack system leads to this and then disappears. A corner now appears above and can be readily bridged all the way to the top. You are now on top of Gribin Facet; work your way up through broken rock to join the path that connects Cwm Idwal with Cwm Bochlwyd and follow this into Cwm Bochlwyd and round Llyn Bochlwyd to the screes below Glyder Fach's main cliff. Identify a feature in the lower centre of the cliff – Alphabet Slabs. Look left of this to the gully that defines its left side – Central Gully. Go into this and, at mid-height, find a large block called the Capstan; Slab Route goes up the rib just to the left of this.

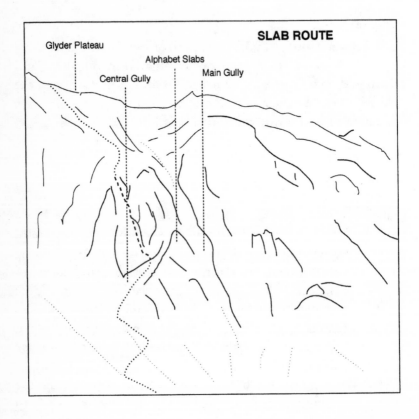

2. Slab Route

CLIMB

Pitch 1: The rib is straightforward and leads to a ledge; belay here.

Pitch 2: The next pitch is less straightforward. Climb up a break in the rock off to the right and then gain an exposed rib-cum-slab that follows a rising traverse to the right. It's delicate and requires a fine sense of balance; the

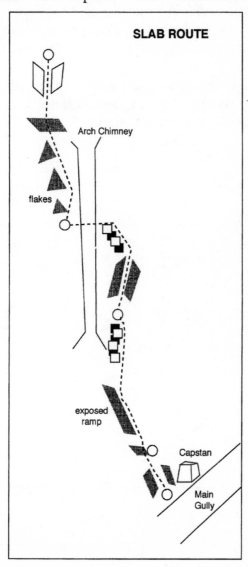

difficulties mount as you climb. At the end of the ramp is a set of slabs off to the right. Climb these to a stance. Belay here.

Pitch 3: You are now to the right of Arch Chimney. Climb a rib on the right of this to get to some more slabs. When they run out traverse left over the chimney, and then belay at the base of some flakes.

Pitch 4: Climb the flakes directly to an exposed ledge – not a place to dawdle – and then gain a shallow corner and the top of the climb. Easy rocks lead to the summit plateau.

DESCENT

There are no straightforward descents down the cliff to the base of the crag. It is better to take in a traverse off the Glyder Plateau and then a scrambling descent of Gribin Ridge.

29. GREAT TOWER BUTTRESS

Mountain: Glyder Fach (994m).

Cliff: East Face of Bristly Ridge.

Location: GR: 660586.

Grade: Severe.

Height: 168m.

Time: 5–6hrs.

Parking: Ogwen Cottage car park; GR: 650603.

Maps: OS Outdoor Leisure (1:25000) sheet 17; OS Landranger (1:50000) sheet 115; Harvey's Map (1:25000 or 1:40000) Snowdonia North.

Guidebook: CC – Ogwen.

Equipment: Either an 11mm or 2 x 9mm rope; a rack including a full range of placements; at least three full-length slings.

Accommodation: Idwal Cottage (Ogwen) YH; tel: (01248) 600225.

INTRODUCTION

Bristly Ridge is one of the best ridge scrambles and most elegant features in Snowdonia. Most of those who ascend it, however, miss out on its best prospect. Tucked away on the Cwm Tryfan side is the ridge's East Face. It's a fascinating collection of sharp, well-defined and shapely pinnacles.

Great Tower Buttress supports the ridge's two outstanding features: Great Tower and Great Tower Gap. The climb of the same name follows an elegant and interesting line directly to its sharp summit. The rock is mostly sound, but a lot more debris has accumulated on its ledges.

Less well known than the neighbouring East Face of Tryfan, climbing here is a relatively lonely experience. The final and exciting moves on to the pinnacle's summit will, however, command an interested audience from the scramblers on the ridge.

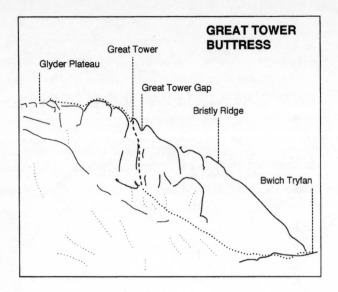

SITUATION

Bristly Ridge sweeps down steeply from the Glyder Plateau to the rocky col at Bwlch Tryfan. From Tryfan the ridge provides an exciting prospect and its direct line is apparent. The East Face consists of a series of steep, well-defined pinnacles and deep gullies that ascend in serried ranks.

Great Tower Buttress is defined on the right by Central Gully and on the left by Brown Gully. It's the Central Gully that forms the very prominent Great Tower Gap. The summit of the buttress forms the isolated pinnacle of Great Tower.

APPROACH

From Ogwen Cottage, follow the major track over the apron of moorland and on up to Cwm Bochlwyd. Continue on the path up to Bwlch Tryfan. Cross the drystone wall at the stile and then traverse round to the south below the rapidly emerging Bristly Ridge. A track cuts below the crags and the best reference point to locating the start of the climb is the bottom of Central Gully. A line of rock flakes rises out of a small bay to the left of the gully; this is the start of the climb.

CLIMB

Pitch 1: Climb the flake-cum-crack easily to gain a short chimney. Above this is some easier ground, above which is a pronounced block. Belay at the base of this.

Pitch 2: The block is split by an obvious – though steep and awkward – crack. Climbing it requires a degree of continuity, but you must get some protection in. It's a thrutch but soon gives way to easier ground at a chimney. Climb the right-hand wall of this to a belay.

Pitch 3: Above this rises a pinnacled arête that provides pleasant climbing and scrambling. It's a full run-out, so don't forget about protection. At the top of the arête is a short but smooth slab that leads to the left. Find some

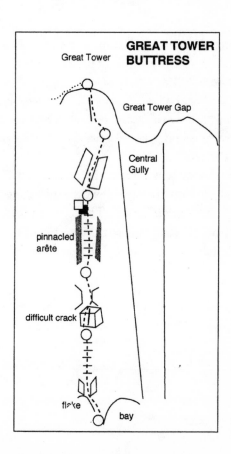

protection before you start on this and climb mostly on friction. Belay once this is cleared.

Pitch 4: Things now get a little more demanding, and this is compounded by a high degree of exposure. Above is a steep and awkward groove – climb this directly and clear a bulge. Once atop this, traverse right to the edge of the buttress and a stance overlooking Central Gully.

Pitch 5: You are now committed high on an exposed buttress and the only line is an exposed crack that splits this facet of the Great Tower. It's more straightforward than it appears, although the situation and the exposure is awesome. You probably won't need reminding to look to placing protection. You emerge directly atop the Great Tower.

DESCENT

The most direct descent is to drop down into Great Tower Gap and descend down Central Gully. The first bit is quite tricky but can be readily abseiled.

To reach the Glyder Plateau, seek out the well-polished line of the scramble and follow this. You are already well up the ridge and all too quickly the steep ground gives way to the wide-open but flat top.

Glyder Fach lies some 400m to the south-west. From here you can opt for a scrambling descent down Gribin Ridge or head back east to pick up the Miners' Track. This cuts back down the screes to the south of Bristly Ridge – providing a grand view of the climb – and on to Bwlch Tryfan and the outward path.

Final pitch of 'C'
Ordinary, Dow
Crag
(Robin Ashcroft)

Esk Buttress looms above
the Great Moss in Upper
Eskdale
(Robin Ashcroft)

ABOVE: Looking out across Langdale from the summit of Pavey Ark
(Tony Shewell)
RIGHT: It's important to be well organised when belaying on a small stance
(Robin Ashcroft)
BELOW: The dramatic skyline of the Langdale Pikes
(Robin Ashcroft)

In Gwynne's Chimney,
Pavey Ark
(Tony Shewell)

Looking out from Grooved
Arête, Pike's Crag
(Robin Ashcroft)

Dealing with the bulge on
Pinnacle Rib, Tryfan's
East Face
(Tony Shewell)

On the final pitch of
Pinnacle Rib, Tryfan's
East Face
(Tony Shewell)

Tryfan's
East Face
(Robin
Ashcroft)

The author with a
comprehensive rack,
bandoleer and
rucksack
(Tony Shewell)

Slab Direct
(Tony Shewell)

The perfect rock of
Idwal Slabs
(Robin Ashcroft)

On the huge expanse
of Idwal Slabs
(Robin Ashcroft)

On the upper section of Cneifion Arête
(Tony Shewell)

On Central Arête, Upper
Cliffs of Glyder Fawr
(Tony Shewell)
INSET: Crib Goch's pinnacles
emerge from the cloud
(Tony Shewell)

Few summits are more isolated – or spectacular –
than Crib Goch's pinnacles
(Robin Ashcroft)

Cneifion Arête
(Robin Ashcroft)

30. CHARITY AND CNEIFION ARÊTE

Mountain: Glyder Fawr (999m).

Cliff: Idwal Slabs and Cneifion Arête.

Location: GR: 645589 and GR: 648587.

Grade: Very Difficult and Moderate
  (Grade 3s) scramble.

Height: 150m and 150m.

Time: 3–5hrs.

Parking: Ogwen Cottage; GR: 649603.

Maps: OS Outdoor Leisure (1:25000)

sheet 17; OS Landranger (1:50000)
  sheet 115; Harvey's Map (1:25000 or
  1:40000) Snowdonia North.

Guidebook: CC – Ogwen

Equipment: 2 x 9mm ropes; a comprehensive rack; at least three full-length
  slings.

Accommodation: Idwal Cottage (Ogwen)
  YH; tel: (01248) 600225.

INTRODUCTION

Idwal Slabs is a stunning piece of rock; its sweep both holds the eye and offers some great climbs. The problem with it is that it is very popular. The trick is to be on it early in the morning and when you reach the top to keep on going. An attractive option is to try to link the slabs with the Upper Cliffs of Glyder Fawr (see Ken Wilson's *Classic Rock*). This, however, is more difficult than is first apparent as all of the short connecting climbs up Holly Tree Wall are technically demanding and exposed – which is completely out of character compared with most of the routes on Idwal Slabs and the Upper Cliff.

Another option is to head on into the remote hanging valley of Cwm Cneifion behind Seniors Ridge. There you will find the Cneifion Arête. This is a classic scramble that is completely alpine in character and provides some uncomplicated mountaineering.

Idwal Slabs provide any number of long routes, but the trio of Faith, Hope and Charity are the most famous and accommodating. Charity is outlined here.

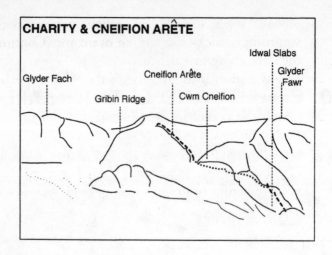

SITUATION

Seniors Ridge descends from the Gribin Plateau and forms the East Wall of Cwm Idwal. Idwal Slabs rise directly from the floor of the valley to mid-height, forming the lower western flank of the ridge. Above them the rock steepens and rears up to Glyder Fach's Upper Cliff.

The slabs are continuous, compact rock, defined on the left by East Wall and on the right by Holly Tree Wall. Charity follows a central and direct line up the main slab.

Cwm Cneifion is behind Seniors Ridge – well above the level of Cwm Idwal and the top of the slabs – and is a classic hanging valley; it is contained to the east by Gribin Ridge and means 'Nameless Valley' in English. Cneifion Arête is a very obvious pinnacled ridge that rises directly off the west wall of Gribin Ridge from the valley floor.

APPROACH

This has to be the easiest approach in the book – a major contributing factor to the ongoing popularity and crowding on the slabs. A veritable 'highway' leads directly from Ogwen Cottage to the base of the slab. Simply follow it.

CLIMB

Pitch 1: Charity follows a central line up the central slab. An obvious crack leads to a shallow groove. Both are surprisingly tricky but can be overcome. Continue up the slabs above to a stance.

Pitch 2: Follow a short rising traverse to the right to the base of a corner. Belay here.

Pitch 3: Climb the corner by bridging; this is straightforward, readily protected and gives way to more slabs. The slabs are followed to the base of another corner. Belay here.

Pitch 4: Climb the corner to yet more slabs. From here you can take numerous routes to the large ledge that marks the top of the slabs.

DESCENT 1

If you wish to return to the base of the slabs then head left and follow the climbers' descent which leads – far from straightforwardly – to a gully. To descend, climb down the gully (it's worth keeping a rope to hand), to go on to Cwm Cneifion, climb up the gully.

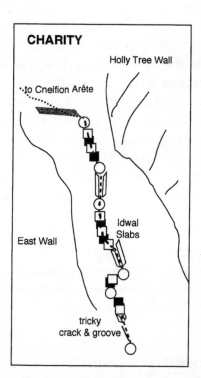

As you enter Cwm Cneifion you will see the very obvious and direct line of Cneifion Arête connecting the valley floor to the top of Gribin Ridge. Its left flank consists of a slabby crag, its right side is a sheer edge. Climb the broken rock to its base.

SCRAMBLE

Pitch 1: To gain the crest of the arête, you need to clear a short rock step. This is exposed and probably deserves a Difficult grade, so pitch it properly. Climb a shallow scoop to a ledge. Belay here.

Pitch 2: A chimney provides access to the crest. Climb into then up this. Belay on the crest.

Pitch 3: Above the crest is pinnacled, exposed and straightforward. It's delightful mountaineering. You can either opt to climb in pitches or move together alpine-fashion. The ridge levels out at the top and joins Gribin Ridge below a large flat area known as the Football Pitch.

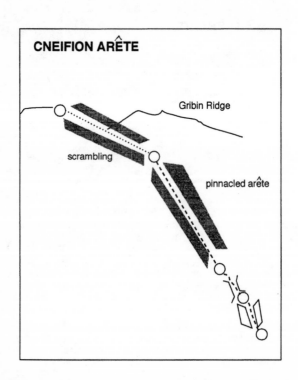

CNEIFION ARÊTE

Gribin Ridge

scrambling

pinnacled arête

DESCENT 2

From the Football Pitch the most direct descent is to head north down the lower section of Gribin Ridge and then drop down into Cwm Idwal.

Gribin Ridge is a delightful grade 1 scramble and its crest leads to the Glyder Plateau. A good option from here is to head west and then cut down the path by the Devil's Kitchen to Llyn Idwal and the outward path.

31. CENTRAL ARÊTE

Mountain: Glyder Fawr (999m).
Cliff: Glyder Fawr – Upper Cliff.
Location: GR: 643585.
Grade: Difficult.
Height: 230m.
Time: 4–6hrs.
Parking: Ogwen Cottage; GR: 649603.
Maps: OS Outdoor Leisure (1:25000)
   sheet 17; OS Landranger (1:50000)

sheet 115; Harvey's (1:25000 and
   1:40000) Snowdonia North.
Guidebook: CC – Ogwen.
Equipment: An 11mm or 2 x 9mm ropes;
   a comprehensive rack, including small
   placements; at least three full-length
   slings.
Accommodation: Idwal Cottage (Ogwen)
   YH; tel: (01248) 600225.

INTRODUCTION

Glyder Fawr's Upper Cliff rears up in splendid isolation, way above the crowds in Idwal and tucked in just below its mountain's summit. Its layered ranks of slabs draw the eye from the valley and they look particularly attractive in the evening sun. Central Arête

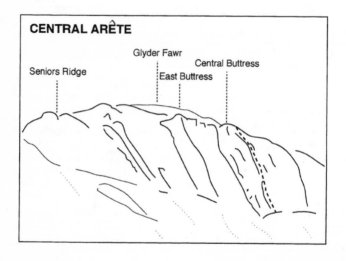

follows a crest formed by the edge of a slab. Its line is direct with a great sense of exposure and isolation.

SITUATION
The Upper Cliffs form the upper flank of Seniors Ridge just below the rim of the Glyder Plateau. Offset from the Idwal Slabs, the climb follows a similar, if steeper, form. Central Arête follows a central line up the crest of a tilted scarp formed by the layers of rock. In its upper reaches the arête is pinnacled but its base is guarded by a steep rock step.

APPROACH
See *30 Charity and Cneifion Arête*, then continue beyond the slabs to a long scree-filled gully. The ascent is direct and tedious but takes you directly to the base of the cliff.

CLIMB
Pitch 1: Central Buttress forms the crag's lowest reaches. Go right of this to the base of the crest formed by the retaining wall on the left and the slabs on the right. Climb some broken rocks and slabs to a large ledge. Belay here.

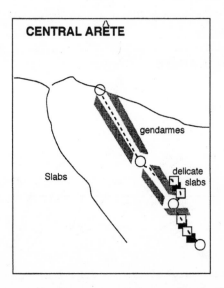

Pitch 2: The arête now becomes more defined and steep. Look to the right-hand side and some slabs that form the edge. Climb this on very delicate holds until you can regain the edge of the arête. Belay in a groove.

Pitch 3: Shift to the left of the arête until a series of 'gendarmes' emerge. Follow these to the top. As there is almost 100m of climbing from here you will need to belay, but there are lots of pinnacles to choose from. Continue over broken ground to the summit plateau.

DESCENT

From the plateau you can descend via the Devil's Kitchen, Bristly Ridge or, most conveniently, Gribin Ridge.

32. CENTRAL ROUTE

Mountain: Carnedd y Filiast (821m).

Cliff: East Face of Carnedd y Filiast.

Location: GR: 623627.

Grade: Difficult.

Height: 300m.

Time: 4–6hrs.

Parking: Tai-Newyddion; GR: 636634.

Maps: OS Outdoor Leisure (1:25000) sheet 17; OS Landranger (1:50000) sheet 115; Harvey's (1:25000 and 1:40000) Snowdonia West.

Guidebook: CC – Ogwen.

Equipment: An 11mm or 2 x 9mm ropes; a comprehensive rack, including small placements; at least three full-length slings.

Accommodation: Idwal Cottage (Ogwen) YH; tel: (01248) 600225.

INTRODUCTION

The slabs of Carnedd y Filiast are spectacular and draw the eye from a long way off. Tucked away in the northern edge of the Glyders they receive a fraction of the attention of the range's central crags. Nevertheless they provide some fine, and novel, climbing.

A series of massive slabs, they rise to over 1,000 feet in places. While the quality of the rock does vary, on Atlantic Slab it is mostly good and is renowned for its 'rippled' texture. As is often the case with slab climbing, the routes tend to be indefinite. Protection can also be scarce, leading to a sense of really being 'out there'.

SITUATION

Layered on top of each other, the slabs drop down in a gentle but continuous sweep from Carnedd y Filiast's main ridge. Central Route follows a relatively direct line up Atlantic Slab – defined by a large corner called the Runnel on the left and on the right by the Ridge – and the ripples providing interesting holds. The route utilises both the slab and the crest at its right edge.

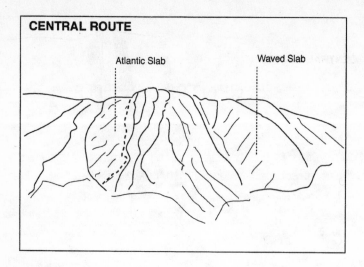

CENTRAL ROUTE

Atlantic Slab   Waved Slab

APPROACH

Leave the old Nant Ffrancon road close by Tai-Newyddion farm and follow the stream which heads south-east into Cwm Graianog. From the lowest point of the slabs a large scree fan descends to meet a drystone wall. The scree leads just to the right of the start of Central Route.

CLIMB

Pitch 1: Start in the middle of the base of the slab and follow a rising traverse to the right using a perch block on the crest as an aiming mark. You will need to set up belays at full rope lengths, but suitable placements are at a premium and these will provide psychological rather than real security. The climbing, however, isn't that difficult and the lack of security is accommodated within the grade. A respite and good belay appear at a ledge and perched block by the edge of the slab.

Pitch 2: From the block you cut back on to the slab and head for the skyline. Again the lack of protection is apparent, but the climbing is straightforward. Just use your sticky soles and keep your hands and heels low.

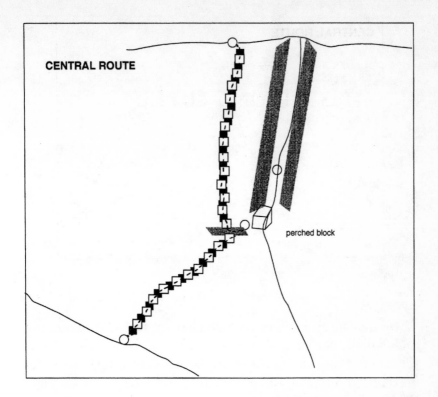

CENTRAL ROUTE

perched block

DESCENT

There are no apparent climbers' descents to the base of the crag. The summit of Carnedd y Filiast is close by, and a walk to Mynidd Perfedd and a descent into Cwm Perfedd is a good option. Do not under any circumstances try to descend by Yr Esgair Ridge: it's a death trap.

33. FLYING BUTTRESS

Mountain: Glyder Fawr (999m).

Cliff: Dinas y Cromlech.

Location: GR: 629568.

Grade: Very Difficult.

Height: 100m.

Time: 3–5hrs.

Parking: Pont y Cromlech; GR: 629566.

Maps: OS Outdoor Leisure (1:25000)
  sheet 17; OS Landranger (1:50000)
  sheet 115; Harvey's (1:25000 and
  1:40000) Snowdonia West.

Guidebook: CC – Llanberis Pass.

Equipment: An 11mm or 2 x 9mm ropes;
  a comprehensive rack, including small
  placements; at least three full-length
  slings.

Accommodation: Pen-y-Pass YH; tel:
  (01286) 872434.

INTRODUCTION

Dinas y Cromlech is one of the most photogenic crags in Snowdonia. The simple geometry of the cliff, focused around the plumb line of Cenotaph Corner, is remarkable. In common with most of the crags on the north side of Llanberis Pass, most of the climbs hereabouts are in the upper grades. Nevertheless, Flying Buttress provides an opportunity to sample this grandeur at a more reasonable level.

SITUATION

Dinas y Cromlech stands on the northern slopes of Llanberis Pass, midway up the flank of Glyder Fawr. The architecture is impressive and is best described as resembling an open book – the lines are exceptionally straight. Flying Buttress is to be found on its more broken right-hand wing. The lower half is a well-defined arête, buttressing the square profile of the upper crag – which is where the climbing gets more complex.

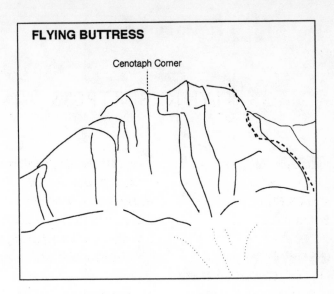

FLYING BUTTRESS

Cenotaph Corner

APPROACH
From the lay-by at Pont y Cromlech head north-west over the open hillside and some small outcrops. Then head directly to the right-hand edge of the crag. The lower ridge is obvious.

CLIMB
Pitch 1: Ascend the ridge directly, utilising a corner in its face. Go to the right of an overhang and belay above this.

Pitch 2: Continue up the ridge to some pinnacles. Belay at the base of those.

Pitch 3: Go left over the pinnacles to a corner-cum-gully, climb this and then follow an exposed traverse to the left. Belay by a flake.

Pitch 4: Climb a steep wall behind the flake to gain a rightward-slanting gangway-cum-slab. Climb this to the base of a chimney and belay there.

Pitch 5: Getting into the chimney is problematic but the climbing eases once you are in. Follow this route to the top.

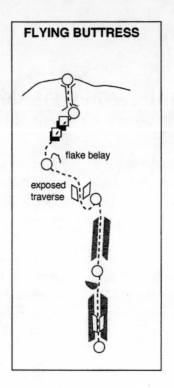

FLYING BUTTRESS

flake belay

exposed
traverse

DESCENT

The most direct descent is to the right, and the path is well marked. Glyder Fawr's summit is some distance above and is reached over steep and uninteresting terrain. In this case the summit can't really be recommended and the best advice is to head for Pen-Y-Gwryd and enjoy a pint.

34. MAIN WALL OF CYRN LAS

Mountain: Crib y Ddysgl (1,065m).

Cliff: Cyrn Las.

Location: GR: 614561.

Grade: Hard Severe.

Height: 145m.

Time: 5–7hrs.

Parking: Blaen-y-Nant; GR: 622570.

Maps: OS Outdoor Leisure (1:25000)
sheet 17; OS Landranger (1:50000)
sheet 115; Harvey's (1:25000 and
1:40000) Snowdonia West.

Guidebook: CC – Llanberis Pass.

Equipment: An 11mm or 2 x 9mm ropes;
a comprehensive rack, including small
placements; at least three full-length
slings and some abseil tape.

Accommodation: Pen-y-Pass YH; tel:
(01286) 872434.

INTRODUCTION

One of the best ways of appreciating the magnificence of Snowdon is to visit the massive cwm formed by Crib y Ddysgl and Crib Goch. The rock architecture is amazing, the atmosphere remote, yet few people – climbers or walkers – see it from here.

The cliffs it contains are not just magnificent but quite beautiful, and Cyrn Las is without doubt the most impressive. It's a serious place, and all of its routes are demanding; not so much on a technical level but on the degree of commitment they require.

Main Wall is the most logical line on the cliff and makes best use of the crag's features. It is rightly described as a classic and should be climbed when you are fit and competent. Then it is a superb expedition.

SITUATION

From the cwm, Cyrn Las is seen as a dome-shaped crag. Its walls are steep and uncompromising and its height is readily apparent. It forms an outlier from Crib y Ddysgl and stands proud, dominating the skyline. The main wall follows a line alongside

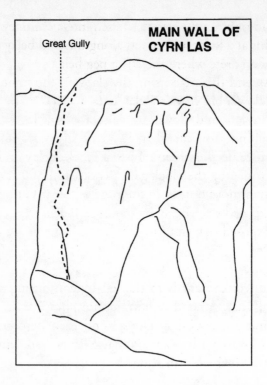

Great Gully and zigzags between the cliff's weaknesses to break through the central section.

APPROACH

From the lay-bys on the A5 near Blaen-y-Nant cross the river and ascend the steep slopes into lower Cwm Glas. Continue along for a little way, then cross the river to approach the left side of the cliff barrier. Climb this by the path to reach upper Cwm Glas. Cyrn Las lies to the north and is approached over a series of terraces and outcrops. Make for the left-hand side of the cliff by Great Gully.

CLIMB

Pitch 1: Identify a triangular overhang about ten metres above the left-hand edge of the ledge. Look below and to the left of this and you will see a broken groove; climb this to a ledge with a spike belay. Belay here.

Pitch 2: Above is a corner, climb this then traverse left to a stance below a rib, with slabs on the right. Belay here.

Pitch 3: Go right up the slabs and then into a chimney. Exit from this at a ledge and go left along this and belay at the base of an arête where there is a peg belay.

Pitch 4: Ascend the arête using the slabs on the right to a ledge below a big corner. Belay here.

Pitch 5: Go left and down to gain a pinnacle with a crack behind. You can then make an awkward and exposed move up the rib and on to a block. Belay on the block.

Pitch 6: From atop the block gain a chockstone-filled groove and then move out on to the edge of Great Gully and up an exposed slab. Belay by the huge block.

Pitch 7: Exposed slabs lead to the summit.

DESCENT

The most direct descent is to the left by contouring round into upper Cwm Glas. A good walking option, however, is to stay on the ridge and go to Crib y Ddysgl and then descend Garnedd Ugain and traverse Crib Goch's Pinnacle Ridge, returning to Cwm Glas via Crib Goch's North Ridge.

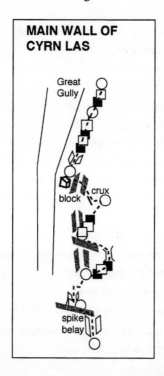

MAIN WALL OF CYRN LAS

Great
Gully

crux

block

spike
belay

35. GAMBIT CLIMB

Mountain: Crib y Ddysgl (1,065m).
Cliff: Clogwyn y Person.
Location: GR: 615553.
Grade: Very Difficult.
Height: 100m.
Time: 5–7hrs.
Parking: Blaen-y-Nant; GR: 622570.
Maps: OS Outdoor Leisure (1:250000)
 sheet 17; OS Landranger (1:50000)
sheet 115; Harvey's (1:25000 and
 1:40000) Snowdonia West.
Guidebook: CC – Llanberis Pass.
Equipment: An 11mm or 2 x 9mm ropes;
 a comprehensive rack, including small
 placements; at least three full-length
 slings and some abseil tape.
Accommodation: Pen-y-Pass YH; tel:
 (01286) 872434.

INTRODUCTION

The Clogwyn y Person arête juts out from Garnedd Ugain in spectacular fashion. Of compact and continuous rock, it is a mountaineer's delight. While the situation is superb, it is a little intimidating; the climbing, however, is actually quite accommodating – and great fun.

Gambit Climb provides varied climbing that can be both athletic and delicate. The protection is sound and the rock mostly good. It's a great introduction to these lonely, but fascinating, high-mountain cirques.

SITUATION

Garnedd Ugain forms a continuous rock barrier between Crib y Ddysgl and Crib Goch. The Clogwyn y Person juts out to the north from this, splitting Cwm Glas from Cwm Ucha. The arête is a whale-back of rock, and Gambit Climb is found on its western flank overlooking Cwm Glas.

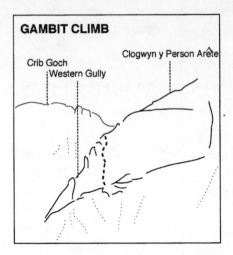

APPROACH

From the lay-bys on the A5 near Blaen-y-Nant, cross the river and ascend the steep slopes into lower Cwm Glas. Continue along for a little way, then cross to approach the left side of the cliff barrier. Climb this by the path and then gain upper Cwm Glas. Walk to Llyn Bach; Clogwyn y Person rises directly above and is reached over a series of terraces.

CLIMB

Pitch 1: At the left side of the terraces, 60m to the right of Western Gully, is a quartz-pocked wall. Start five metres to the left of this in a broken corner. Climb the corner to some slabs, then traverse left to the bottom of a crack. Climb this to a ledge. A short corner then leads to a stance. Belay here.

Pitch 2: Climb a block-filled groove to a ledge. Belay here.

Pitch 3: A tricky and exposed traverse to the right leads to the base of a chimney, which provides a welcome respite. Climb this to a ledge and move left to a pinnacle. Belay here.

Pitch 4: A chimney behind the pinnacle is climbed, exit this and then follow a hand traverse to the right to gain a corner and a belay stance.

Pitch 5: Follow a sloping ledge to the right to gain access to a

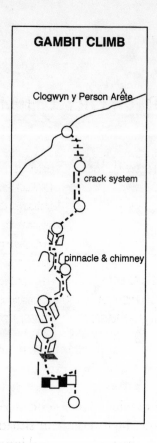

narrow crack system, from here a series of strenuous moves leads to a belay.

Pitch 6:   Scramble to the crest of the arête.

DESCENT

To return to Cwm Glas, descend the arête to Western Gully. This can be tricky and a rope is useful. To take in a summit, go up the ridge to Garnedd Ugain and scramble to Crib y Ddysgl. A descent down the Snowdon zigzags isn't that convenient as you'll have a long walk along the road if you need to return to your start point. A better option is to traverse Crib Goch's Pinnacle Ridge and then descend by the North Ridge.

36. RECTORY CHIMNEYS

Mountain: Crib y Ddysgl (1,065m).

Cliff: Clogwyn y Person.

Location: GR: 615553.

Grade: Very Difficult.

Height: 100m.

Time: 5–7hrs.

Parking: Blaen-y-Nant; GR: 622570.

Maps: OS Outdoor Leisure (1:25000)
   sheet 17; OS Landranger 91:50000)

sheet 115; Harvey's (1:25000 and
   1:40000) Snowdonia West.

Guidebook: CC – Llanberis Pass.

Equipment: An 11mm or 2 x 9mm ropes;
   a comprehensive rack including small
   placements; at least three full-length
   slings and some abseil tape.

Accommodation: Pen-y-Pass YH; tel:
   (01286) 872434.

INTRODUCTION
Rectory Chimneys provides some good – Very Difficult grade – climbing in a remote, high-mountain situation. The climbing is very straightforward, although it can feel intimidating. As with the two previous routes, the location is part of the attraction.

SITUATION
See *35 Gambit Climb*. Rectory Chimneys utilises a series of chimneys that breach the crag at its highest point.

APPROACH
See *35 Gambit Climb*.

CLIMB
Pitch 1: At the right side of the terraces is a chimney blocked by a flake. Use the flake to get into, and then climb, the chimney. Belay at the top.

Pitch 2: Climb a short, steep wall, then use a corner to approach the base of a pinnacle; a crack and mantleshelf provide

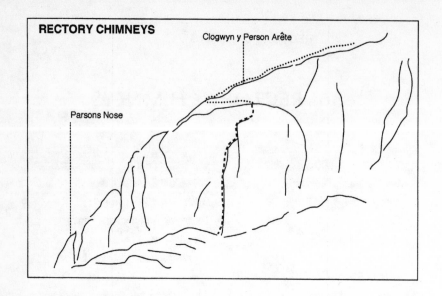

access to a niche at the base of the chimney.

Pitch 3: Go left and round the back of the pinnacle and climb easily to a belay stance.

Pitch 4: Climb a corner, then step into a chimney. Climb this to a belay stance.

Pitches 5 and 6: A wide traverse leads across the top of a gully and on to a ramp which follows a rising traverse to another chimney. Belay at the base of this.

Pitch 7: Climb the chimney to easy rocks and the crest of the arête.

DESCENT
See *35 Gambit Climb*.

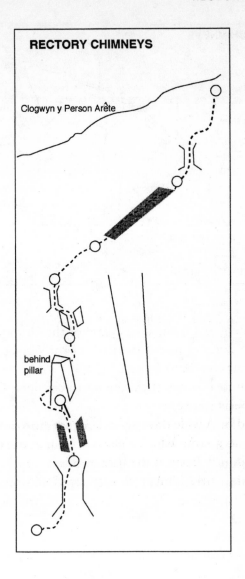

RECTORY CHIMNEYS

Clogwyn y Person Arête

behind
pillar

37. READE'S ROUTE

Mountain: Crib Goch (923m).

Cliff: North Face of Crib Goch; Crib Goch
   Buttress.

Location: GR: 625553.

Grade: Very Difficult.

Height: 85m.

Time: 4–6hrs.

Parking: Blaen-y-Nant; GR: 622570.

Maps: OS Outside Leisure (1:25000)
   sheet 17; OS Landranger (1:50000)

sheet 115; Harvey's Map (1:25000 or
   1:40000) Snowdonia West.

Guidebook: CC – Llanberis Pass

Equipment: Either an 11mm or 2 x 9mm
   ropes and a rack including a full range
   of placements; at least three full-
   length slings.

Accommodation: Pen-y-Pass YH; tel:
   (01286) 872434.

INTRODUCTION

Crib Goch's Pinnacle Ridge and its pinnacles are rightly regarded as the best part of the Snowdon Horseshoe. It's a classic mountaineering traverse, yet this aspect of the mountain often overshadows everything else it has to offer. It's not until you get into the remote vastness of Cwm Glas and Cwm Uchaf that you really see what a grand mountain it is.

Yet Crib Goch is only part of the picture, for it forms but one aspect of the most magnificent high-mountain cirque that Snowdonia possesses. The panorama that starts at Crib Goch's eastern – and subsidiary summit – sweeps round, taking in the pinnacles; on to Garnedd Ugain and its Clogwyn y Person arête; to Crib y Ddysgl and finally to Carn Las.

Nevertheless, Crib Goch Buttress remains the single most outstanding feature in the panorama. A straight, clean needle of rock that rises proudly above its scree in one sweep. Reade's Route will take you up this and the backdrop has few equals in all of Britain's mountains.

SITUATION

Crib Goch forms the southern curtain of the Cwm Glas–Cwm Uchaf cirque. It has three ridges: the North, East and Pinnacle Ridge. However, it's Pinnacle Ridge that effectively forms the mountain. It's a long, narrow arête running roughly east–west. The eastern two-thirds are made up of a razor-sharp edge, the western third of three pinnacles.

The northern flanks of the pinnacles are steep, and it is from this side that Reade's Route rises to the summit of the highest of the three pinnacles. This, however, isn't the mountain's summit – this lies midway down the knife edge, a barely perceptible rising that is usually ignored.

APPROACH

See *36 Rectory Chimneys*. Then traverse around to the south to Llyn Glas and on to some unnamed pools in Cwm Uchaf. A faint path winds up the scree to the rock at the base of Crib Goch Buttress. Identify Crazy Pinnacle Gully and go to the rocks at the left of its base.

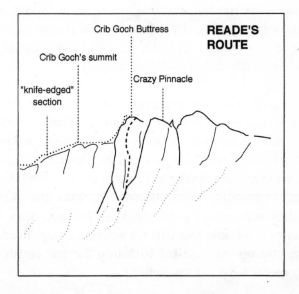

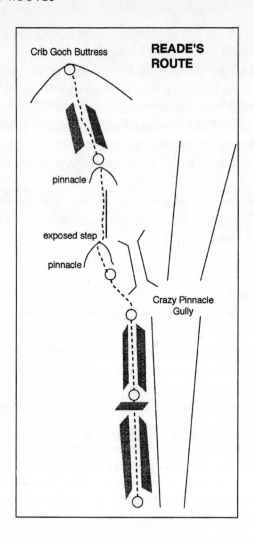

Crib Goch Buttress

READE'S ROUTE

pinnacle

exposed step

pinnacle

Crazy Pinnacle Gully

CLIMB

Pitch 1: The first scramble is up broken, slabby ground then it steepens and you can belay at a stance overlooking Crazy Pinnacle Gully; the climbing proper starts here. A broken rib to the left of the gully leads on up. This is broken by several ledges, all of which can be used as subsidiary belay stances. The rib comes to an end where Crazy Pinnacle Gully splits. Go left up a ramp into the left-hand chimney-cum-gully. Belay here.

Pitch 2: Look to the left and climb a steep wall, with one difficult move to the left to gain a belay at the base of a pinnacle. Belay here.

Pitch 3: Climb the pinnacle directly and on to its top. Now follows the crux. A committing stride is needed from the pinnacle to a crack on the far wall. It should be protected before you commit yourself, but take care to minimise drag. The crack leads directly up the front of a second pinnacle. Belay at the top of this in a snug stance.

Pitch 4: A rib leads to the top of the buttress and on to Crib Goch Pinnacle. Snowdonian summits don't often come more alpine-like than this.

DESCENT

The most direct descent is down Western Gully. This is reached by heading westwards over Bwlch Coch and then down the screes into Cwm Uchaf. Other options include the remainder of the Snowdon Horseshoe which, despite the prominence of Crib Goch, still has some good scrambling to come; particularly the Garnedd Ugain section and the ascent of Lliwedd. The problem with this is that you will get off the mountain a long way from your start point.

The climb, however, belongs to Crib Goch, so a good way is to head east over the knife edge, take in the summit and then descend back down into Cwm Uchaf via the North Ridge. This is separate from the classic Horseshoe route, but is a grand grade one scramble and a lot more convenient than the East Ridge. The North Ridge terminates in Cwm Uchaf and you can readily pick up your outward path.

38. SLANTING BUTTRESS

Mountain: Lliwedd (898m).

Cliff: Slanting Buttress.

Location: GR: 622535.

Grade: Difficult.

Height: 225m.

Time: 6–8hrs.

Parking: Pen-y-Pass; GR: 647556.

Maps: OS Outside Leisure (1:250000) sheet 17; OS Landranger (1:50000) sheet 115; Harvey's (1:25000 and 1:40000) Snowdonia West.

Guidebook: CC – Lliwedd.

Equipment: 2 x 9mm ropes; a comprehensive rack including small placements; at least three full-length slings and tape for an abseil anchor.

Accommodation: Pen-y-Pass YH; tel (01286) 872434.

INTRODUCTION

Lliwedd is the finest cliff in either Snowdonia or the Lake District for mountaineering rock-climbs. It's a face of alpine proportions and brings both the problems and delights that this involves. Any expedition on this crag is a serious undertaking, irrespective of the grade.

Slanting Buttress is probably the most straightforward of the continuous climbs, and is the best introduction to these cliffs. It follows a rising traverse up Slanting Buttress, the most westerly of the mountain's cliffs. The main challenge lies not in its technical difficulty, but in adjusting to the scale of the undertaking, route-finding and the risk from stone fall.

SITUATION

Lliwedd has four principal buttresses: Far-east Buttress, East Buttress, West Buttress and Slanting Buttress – all rise to over the 300m mark. Slanting Buttress is the most westerly and, as its name suggests, lies at an angle, abutting West Buttress and Lliwedd's main summit.

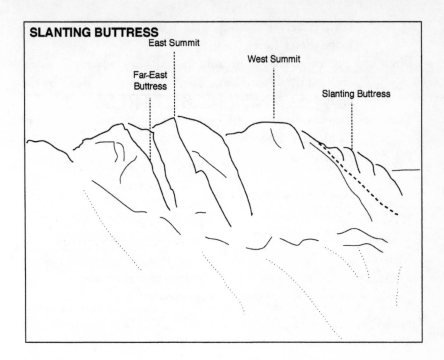

APPROACH

From the car park at Pen-y-Pass, follow the Miners' Track to Llyn Llydaw. From here the Lliwedd cliffs are obvious and are best approached along the left-hand shore. Follow an obvious rising track that skirts below the cliff and up the scree. Go to the base of Slanting Buttress and look for two zigzag quartz marks. The climb starts between these.

CLIMB

Pitches 1 and 2: Scramble up easy ground past a pile of rocks – possibly belay – and on to the base of a corner. Belay here.

Pitch 3: Follow a rising traverse below and beyond the corner on the left. Then go towards the edge of Slanting Gully to reach a recess. Belay here.

Pitch 4: Go up the recess and on to the edge of the gully and belay at the base of a ridge.

Pitch 5: Go to the left side of the ridge and climb up a series of corners before cutting back right on to the crest of the ridge. Belay here.

Pitch 6: The ridge now levels out and you can traverse its edge. It is exposed, so take care with protection. Belay at the end of this.

Pitch 7: Traverse right across a grassy edge to gain the bottom of a chimney. Belay here.

Pitch 8: Ahead lies the crux; climb the chimney and then step left to gain a second chimney-cum-groove and then belay at the base of a slab.

Pitch 9: Climb the slabs and then go left to gain the front of the ridge and then go around this further to the left to gain a corner-chimney system that leads to the summit.

DESCENT

You are now on the best-known ridge traverse in Snowdonia – the Snowdon Horseshoe. Depending on time, you may be able to take in Snowdon's summit and then traverse Crib Goch's Pinnacle Ridge.

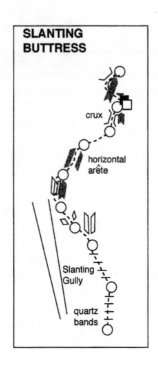

The chances are, however, that you will already have had a long day, so it is more practical to recommend taking in Lliwedd's main summit and then follow the Snowdon Horseshoe to the east, over Lliwedd Bach and then back down to Llyn Llydaw and the Miners' Track.

39. AVALANCHE, RED WALL AND LONGLAND'S CONTINUATION

Mountain: Lliwedd (898m).
Cliff: East Buttress.
Location: GR: 625534.
Grade: Very Difficult and Hard Very Difficult.
Height: 290m.
Time: 6–8hrs.
Parking: Pen-y-Pass; GR: 647556.
Maps: OS Outdoor Leisure (1:25000) sheet 17; OS Landranger (1:50000) sheet 115; Harvey's (1:25000 and 1:40000) Snowdonia West.
Guidebook: CC – Lliwedd.
Equipment: 2 x 9mm ropes; a comprehensive rack including small placements; at least three full-length slings and tape for an abseil anchor.
Accommodation: Pen-y-Pass YH; tel: (01286) 872434.

INTRODUCTION

This combination of climbs follows a superb line up the front of Lliwedd's East Buttress. It is a major undertaking that bears little relation to its modest grade. It isn't that the climbing is technically difficult; it's the size of the cliff and the length of the climb. As a result this is a climb best left until you have experience of long routes.

SITUATION

East Buttress is one of the two major central buttresses which supports the mountain's second summit. The route links together three climbs: Avalanche, Red Wall and Longland's Continuation, and utilises a number of major features on the cliff – including a long but easy traverse at mid-height below Great Terrace. While the rock is mostly sound, there is a fair amount of stone fall from the ridge above.

APPROACH

See *38 Slanting Buttress* but go to the base of East Buttress. It is worth identifying Heather Terrace during the approach.

1. Avalanche

CLIMB

Pitch 1: Scramble to Heather Terrace; this can be difficult if the rock is wet and should be pitched. Go to the right end of the ledge and belay there.

Pitch 2: Traverse right over a rib, across a corner and then across and up a second rib. Follow a rising traverse up to some slabs, go over these up to a stance. Belay here.

Pitch 3: Go up some more slabs to a ledge. Belay here.

Pitch 4: Things now become more problematic. Climb a steep, quartz-pocked wall to gain a ledge and then step to the left side to gain a corner. Climb this with some difficulty to a stance. Belay here.

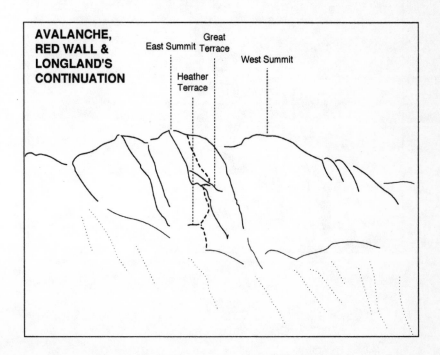

AVALANCHE,
RED WALL &
LONGLAND'S
CONTINUATION

East Summit Great Terrace

West Summit

Heather Terrace

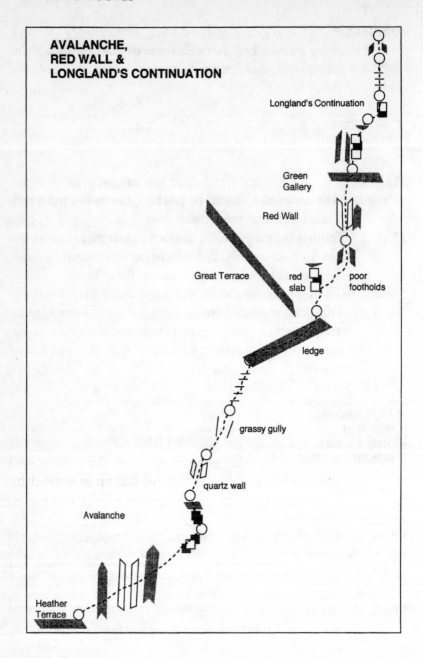

**AVALANCHE,
RED WALL &
LONGLAND'S CONTINUATION**

Longland's Continuation

Green
Gallery

Red Wall

Great Terrace

red
slab

poor
footholds

ledge

grassy gully

quartz wall

Avalanche

Heather
Terrace

Pitches 5, 6 and 7: A grassy gully and easy ground leads to a large ledge below Great Terrace. A 40m scramble to the right-hand edge of the ledge leads to the base of a red slab. Belay here.

2. Red Wall

CLIMB

Pitch 1: The route now heads on up the slabs until your way is barred by an overhang. This forces you out right on poor footholds and a high degree of commitment until you can gain an arête and continue on up. Continue easily to a ledge. Belay here.

Pitch 2: Continue on up the rib, making use of a corner to the left. This gives way to easy ground and Green Gallery. Belay here.

3. Longland's Continuation

CLIMB

Pitch 1: Go right to some quartz-sprinkled rocks four metres to the left of a gully. Climb up a rib then move to a jammed block to the right-hand side on to some slabs. Climb these and then move up over a bulge to a stance. Belay here.

Pitch 2: Go right on to some slabs and up these to a stance. Belay here.

Pitch 3: Climb some splintered rocks easily to gain a ledge. Belay here.

Pitch 4: Above is a slabby rib. Start this from up a thin crack in the centre and then continue up the front of the nose or on easier ground to the left. The going eases and you gain Lliwedd's eastern summit.

DESCENT
See *38 Slanting Buttress*.

40. HORNED CRAG

Mountain: Lliwedd (898m).
Cliff: East Buttress.
Location: GR: 626533.
Grade: Hard Very Difficult.
Height: 260m.
Time: 6–8hrs.
Parking: Pen-y-Pass; GR: 647556.
Maps: OS Outside Leisure (1:25000) sheet 17; OS Landranger (1:50000) sheet 115; Harvey's (1:25000 and 1:40000) Snowdonia North.
Guidebook: CC – Lliwedd.
Equipment: 2 x 9mm ropes; a comprehensive rack including small placements; at least three full-length slings and tape for an abseil anchor.
Accommodation: Pen-y-Pass YH; tel: (01286) 872434.

INTRODUCTION
Another major mountaineering expedition on Lliwedd's East Face. Again the situations are superb, but this time with more technically demanding climbing. Particular attention must be paid to route-finding.

SITUATION
See *38 Slanting Buttress*. Horned Crag is part of the East Buttress and follows a remarkably direct and continuous line. Again the starting point is Heather Terrace, but this time it trends left, making best use of the features overlooking East Gully.

APPROACH
See *39 Avalanche, Red Wall and Longland's Continuation*, but go via the left-hand end of Heather Terrace.

CLIMB
Pitch 1: Scramble to Heather Terrace; this can be difficult if the

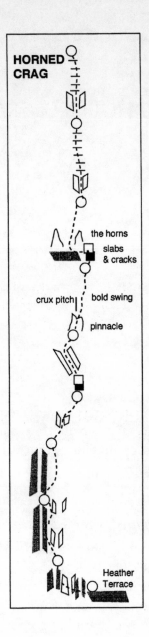

HORNED CRAG

the horns

slabs & cracks

crux pitch | bold swing

pinnacle

Heather Terrace

rock is wet and should be pitched. Go to the left end of the ledge and belay there.

Pitch 2: Traverse left over a rib, corner to a second rib, climb this directly to gain a stance below a rib. Belay here.

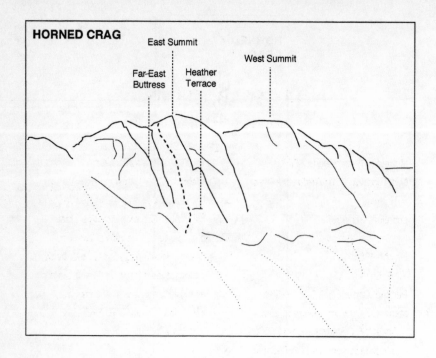

Pitch 3: Climb the steep corner to the right of the rib before cutting back on to the front of the arête and then back into the corner. Belay at a stance.

Pitch 4: Trend right up another corner to belay at the base of some slabs.

Pitch 5: Climb the slabs to gain a corner and then climb to the base if a pinnacle. Belay here.

Pitch 6: Climb above the pinnacle and into a crack line. A bold swing to the right leads to easier going and a stance on a ledge. Belay here.

Pitch 7: Climb some slabs to a large ledge and then climb between the two 'horns' and up a steep climb up to a good stance.

Pitches 8 and 9: Easy rocks to lead on to the summit.

DESCENT
See 38 Slanting Buttress.

41. SLAB CLIMB

Mountain: Snowdon (1,085m).
Cliff: Clogwynn Du'r Arrdu – Far-west Buttress.
Location: GR: 599556.
Grade: Hard Severe.
Height: 155m.
Time: 5–7hrs.
Parking: Cader Ellyll; GR: 582589.
Maps: OS Outdoor Leisure (1:25000) sheet 17; OS Landranger (1:50000) sheet 115; Harvey's (1:25000 and 1:40000) Snowdonia West.
Guidebook: CC – Clogwynn Du'r Arrdu.
Equipment: 2 x 9mm x 45m ropes; a comprehensive rack including small placements; a selection of pitons in case an *in-situ* peg is missing or badly rusted; at least three full-length slings and tape for an abseil anchor.
Accommodation: Llanberis YH; tel (01286) 870280.

INTRODUCTION

Clogwynn Du'r Arrdu – or 'Cloggy' – is generally regarded as being the most technically demanding cliff in Snowdonia. It has a tremendous tradition as the forcing ground of new techniques and in pushing grades. It's also a magnificent piece of rock – the slabs of Western Buttress are superb – and a fine, high-mountain cliff with few equals. While there is little in the lower grades, what there is is quite superb. Of note are the two Slab Climbs on Far-west Buttress; of the two, Right-Hand is probably the best.

SITUATION

Clogwynn Du'r Arrdu lies to the north-west of Snowdon Summit at the head of Cwm Brwynnog. The commanding feature of Cloggy is, without doubt, the slabs of the Western Buttress. All of the routes on it are both serious and technical. West Buttress lies to the right of this and below the rising traverse of the Steep Band. It's roughly diamond-shaped and is defined on the left by Slanting

Chimney and on the right by Deep Chimney. The Slab Climb – Right-Hand – follows the right-hand edge of the slabs overlooking Deep Gully.

APPROACH
From Cader Ellyll follow the Llanberis Path alongside the railway, then a kilometre beyond Halfway House Station take the right-hand fork which leads to the base of the scree. A path skirts round the lake and can be followed to the bottom of the Far-west Buttress.

CLIMB
Pitch 1: The first pitch is a full run-out and is found just to the left of the bottom of Deep Chimney and the base of the buttress. Traverse right using a series of sloping gantries to gain a corner and then the base of some slabs. Climb these directly to a good stance by a spike. Belay here.

Pitch 2: Follow a grassy rake left until it is possible to climb up right to gain the base of a large slab. Climb this easily to a good stance on a ledge. Belay placements are limited and you will need to use an in-situ peg.

Pitch 3: Climb diagonally left to gain the edge of slabs as it over-looks Deep Chimney. The situation is sensational. Look to protection as an unprotected fall would be serious

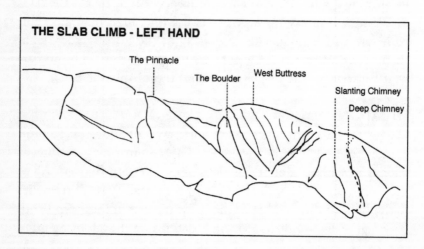

THE SLAB CLIMB - LEFT HAND

The Pinnacle

The Boulder   West Buttress

Slanting Chimney

Deep Chimney

and there isn't an overabundance of placements. Small 'Rocks' seem to offer most potential. At a full run-out, belay in the chimney.

Pitch 4: Move back left on to easier but still exposed ground on the slab. This is shared with Slab Climb – Left-Hand. Pick out the easiest line and belay at the base of an arête.

Pitch 5: Scramble up the arête to complete the climb on top of Far-western Terrace.

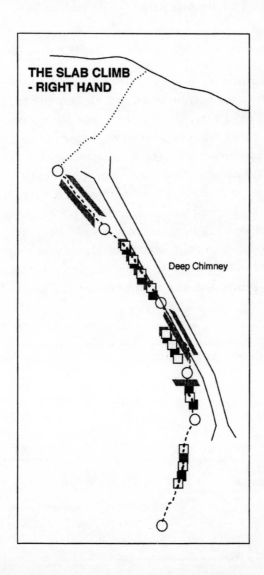

THE SLAB CLIMB
- RIGHT HAND

Deep Chimney

DESCENT

It is possible to descend left down Far-western Terrace but, due to loose rock, this is dangerous. It is better to use the upper section of the terrace to gain the main ridge and then skirt round to the right of the crag – clearing it completely – before coming back along its base.

Snowdon Summit is easily gained via the Snowdon Ranger path and then the only viable return to your start point is by the 'motorway' of the Llanberis path.

42. CENTRAL RIDGE

Mountain: Snowdon (1,085m).
Cliff: Llechogg – Western Cliff.
Location: GR: 597537.
Grade: Difficult.
Height: 120m.
Time: 5–7hrs.
Parking: Car park at Snowdon Ranger;
  GR: 564500.
Maps: OS Outdoor Leisure (1:25000)
  sheet 17; OS Landranger (1:50000)
sheet 115; Harvey's (1:25000 and
  1:40000) Snowdonia Central.
Guidebook: CC – Tremadog and Cwm
  Silyn.
Equipment: Either a single 11mm or 2 x
  9mm ropes; a comprehensive rack; at
  least three full-length slings.
Accommodation: Snowdon Ranger YH;
  tel: (01286) 650391.

INTRODUCTION
The southern side of Snowdon sees a fraction of the attention that its Llanberis Pass flank receives. Although the climbing isn't of the same very high standard of that found to the north, there is still a wealth of potential for the mountaineering rock-climber.

Llechogg is a major cliff by any definition and Central Ridge utilises one of the cliff's most important features. The climbing is good and the rock is sound on this route – although that isn't the case for the whole cliff. The climbing is straightforward and simple, and you can vary the route pretty well much at will.

SITUATION
Llechogg forms Cwm Clogwynn's south-west wall. The cwm itself is a massif cirque high up on Snowdon's western flank and directly below its summit. The cliff trends north-west to south-east and is broken in places. Central Ridge lies just to the right of the very obvious feature of Central Gully.

APPROACH

Follow the well-marked Snowdon Ranger path to the reservoir at Llyn Ffynnon-y-gwas. Skirt round its southern shore to cross the Afon Goch to Llyn Coch. The cliff, its features and the climb, are now easily seen and approached over broken ground.

CLIMB

Pitches 1 and 2: Go to the base of Central Gully; just to the right is the base of an arête. The climb starts here. The first section of the ridge ascends for an unbroken 60m. The climbing is continuous but straightforward and can be pitched at will. Two reasonable run-outs will see you to a large grassy ledge. Belay here.

Pitch 3: Traverse right to gain a vegetated chimney, climb this and then cut back left to gain the main crest. Follow this until your way is barred by an overhang. Belay here.

Pitch 4: Go right or left to clear the overhang and then continue on up the ridge to the top.

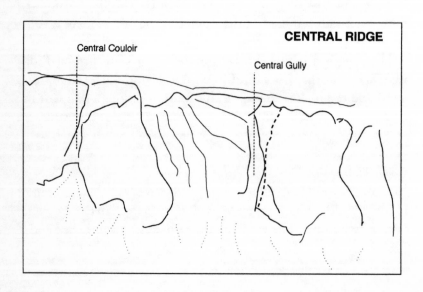

DESCENT

The most direct descent lies to the left down Central Couloir. To take in Snowdon Summit, pick up the Rhyd-ddu Path and follow this over the rugged walk and some simple scrambling of Bwlch Main. From the summit drop down to the marker stone at Bwlch Glas and pick up the Snowdon Ranger path.

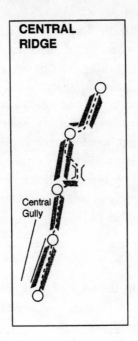

43. SUNSET RIB AND ARTIST'S CLIMB

Mountain: Carnedd Silyn (734m).
Cliff: Craig yr Ogof – Cwm Silyn.
Location: GR: 517501.
Grade: Difficult.
Height: 165m.
Time: 5–7hrs.
Parking: Bryn Gwyn; GR: 496511.
Maps: OS Outdoor Leisure (1:25000)
sheet 17; OS Landranger (1:50000)
sheet 115.

Guidebook: CC – Tremadog and Cwm
Silyn.
Equipment: Either a single 11mm or 2 x
9mm ropes; a comprehensive rack; at
least three full-length slings.
Accommodation: Snowdon Ranger YH;
tel: (01286) 650391.

INTRODUCTION

Cwm Silyn lies well to the west of, and is remote from, the main climbing area in North Wales, and peace and quiet are always possible here. The cwm forms a giant scoop out of the picturesque Nantlle Ridge which, despite the ravages of the slate quarries, has great charm.

The cliffs that make up the back of the cwm are all impressive, but without doubt the best is Craig yr Ogof – if only for the quality of the rock. It holds several classic Welsh rock-climbs and has good climbing at all grades.

Sunset Rib is a classic Welsh Difficult that unfortunately ends well below the summit ridge. It can, however, be connected with some scrambling and the less well-endowed Artist's Climb to make a great expedition.

SITUATION

Craig yr Ogof appears as a giant fang to the left of centre of the broad sweep of Cwm Silyn's cliffs. Its most obvious features are the

Great Slab, which forms the cliff's right-hand facet, and the arête which rises above it and to the left – the Nose.

Sunset Rib connects the lowest point of the crag with a system of ledges at mid-height; the Sunset Ledge–Ogof Terrace. A significant section of scrambling, using a broken gully to the left, leads to the base of the Nose and a straightforward, if airy, climax over the pinnacles of Artist's Climb. It's good, uncomplicated stuff.

APPROACH
While it is permissible to park your car on the road, please do take care that it is not causing an obstruction in the narrow country lanes. Follow the track up to the twin lakes of Cwm Silyn and up the scree to the base of the crag.

1. Sunset Rib

CLIMB
Pitch 1: Go to a rib at the lowest point of the crag and climb this directly to a vegetated ledge. Belay here.

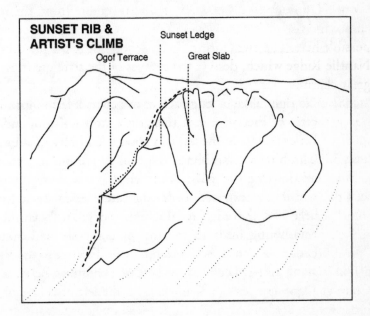

SUNSET RIB & ARTIST'S CLIMB
Sunset Ledge
Ogof Terrace   Great Slab

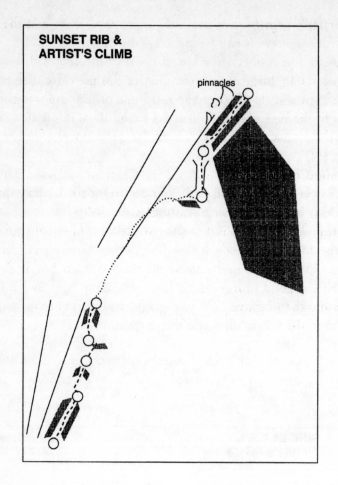

SUNSET RIB & ARTIST'S CLIMB

pinnacles

Pitch 2: Go right along a ledge and then cut back left to gain the crest of the ridge and then right to a series of spikes. Follow these on the left to a good spike belay in a notch.

Pitch 3: Climb over scrambling-cum-broken ground to a stance overlooking the gully. Belay here.

Pitch 4: Climb the exposed knife-edge arête easily to a good belay on the edge overlooking the gully. Belay here. Scrambling leads to the top of the gully and Sunset Ledge via a crack behind a pinnacle. Traverse to the right along Sunset Ledge to the base of a chimney. Belay here.

2. Artist's Climb

CLIMB
Pitch 1: Climb the chimney to the crest of the ridge. Belay here.
Pitch 2: Gain the crest of the ridge and follow this – traversing some large pinnacles to the top.

DESCENT
The most direct descent is down the Great Stone Shoot. This lies well to the right of Craig yr Ogof and the path is apparent but shouldn't be confused with Amphitheatre Gully.

Great ridge walking rather than isolated, mountainous summits are the forte of Nantlle Ridge. The logical summit is Carnedd Silyn (734m); this isn't named on the OS map but is at GR: 526503. A good round can be had by heading over Bwlch Drosbern and then Mynydd Tal-y-mignedd and then contouring back round to the Cwm Silyn and the outward path.

44. OUTSIDE EDGE

Mountain: Carnedd Silyn (734m).
Cliff: Craig yr Ogof – Cwm Silyn.
Location: GR: 517501.
Grade: Hard Very Difficult.
Height: 125m.
Time: 5–7hrs.
Parking: Bryn Gwyn; GR: 496511.
Maps: OS Outdoor Leisure (1:25000)
sheet 17; OS Landranger (1:50000)
sheet 115.

Guidebook: CC – Tremadog and Cwm
Silyn.
Equipment: Either a single 11mm or 2 x
9mm ropes; a comprehensive rack; at
least three full-length slings.
Accommodation: Snowdon Ranger YH;
tel: (01286) 650391.

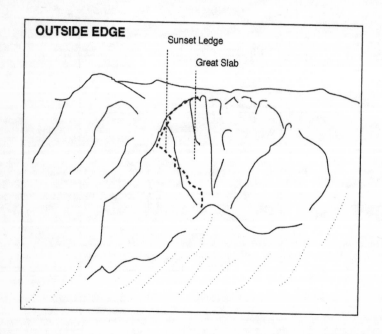

OUTSIDE EDGE

Sunset Ledge

Great Slab

INTRODUCTION
A stupendous route that, although sharing some common ground in the upper reaches with *43 Sunset Rib and Artist's Climb*, takes in some superbly exposed moves on the outside edge of the Great Slab. The climbing is well within grade and readily protected, but the situation is often one of great exposure.

SITUATION
The Great Slab forms the northern facet of Craig yr Ogof. This route follows a circular line around its left-hand open edge – and then joins the Nose to come back over the top of itself.

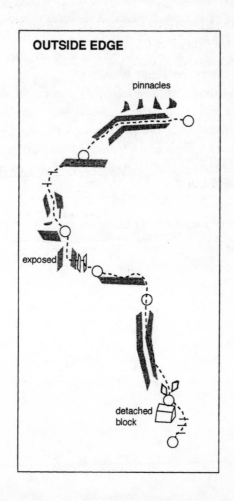

APPROACH
See *43 Sunset Rib and Artist's Climb*. Go five metres to the right of the left-hand edge of the slab and below an obvious detached hanging block.

CLIMB
Pitch 1: Scramble to the detached block and climb behind it and to the right. Belay on the block.

Pitch 2: Climb steeply into an awkward niche and then follow a rising traverse to the left to an exposed arête. Climb this directly to a stance below a large terrace – Sunset Ledge. Belay here.

Pitch 3: Traverse along the ledge and belay by a groove.

Pitch 4: The crux now appears. A delicate traverse leads out left over a corner, then a rib and then a tricky corner and a final rib. This should be climbed to reach a good stance on the ledge. Belay here.

Pitch 5: Continue trending left until you can climb to the right of a bulge and then gain a wide and awkward crack. Above is a rib, followed by easier ground where you join Artist's Climb and Ordinary Route. Belay at a ledge.

Pitch 6: An exposed but pinnacled arête leads to the top.

DESCENT
See *43 Sunset Rib and Artist's Climb*.

45. CYFRWY ARÊTE

Mountain: Cader Idris.	sheet 23; OS Landranger (1:50000)
Cliff: Cyfrwy Arête.	sheet 124.
Location: GR: 705135.	Guidebook: CC – Mid-Wales.
Grade: Difficult.	Equipment: Either a single 11mm or 2 x
Height: 175m.	9mm ropes; a comprehensive rack; at
Time: 4–6hrs.	least three full-length slings.
Parking: Car park; GR: 698152.	Accommodation: Kings (Dolgellau) YH;
Maps: OS Outdoor Leisure (1:25000)	tel: (01341) 422392.

INTRODUCTION

Cyfrwy Arête played a particularly poignant part in the history of mountaineering and rock-climbing. It was the first route ever undertaken by Owen Glynne Jones, a man at least as significant to the story of rock-climbing as W.P. Haskett-Smith (the first climber of Napes Needle).

In 1888, O.G. Jones was an adventurous young man but had no experience of mountaineering. When he saw the prominent Cyfrwy Arête – it's certainly a route that draws the eye – he climbed it on impulse. That he soloed it in smooth, leather-soled boots speaks volumes for his determination and skill, if not perhaps his sense of self-preservation!

He went on to do great things, interestingly, mostly in the Lake District rather than in his native Wales. His later routes were far in advance of what was being climbed at that time and have remained test-piece climbs for many years.

On Cyfrwy Arête you can sense the freedom he must have felt in simply climbing a route. It remains a superb outing, never too serious – assuming you're roped – but always thrilling. It's also an incredibly beautiful piece of mountain architecture. Tragically, O.G. Jones died in an accident in the Alps in 1899.

SITUATION

Cader Idris's northern cliffs follow a line of over three miles – very impressive and one of the longest cliffs in Snowdonia. Its line is really broken only once by the cwm of Llyn y Gadair. Cyfrwy Arête rises directly above this, a classic arête, alpine in character and unmistakable from the moment you clear the woodline.

Cyfrwy Arête's serrated crest rises in a series of towers, the ascent of which are graded as either a 3S scramble or a Moderate rock-climb. To liven things up, however, you can opt for a direct ascent of the Table – the lower tower – by climbing Table Direct and then continuing on up to the summit plateau atop an airy scrambling ridge.

APPROACH

Leave the road and follow the marked Pony Path up through the trees. After 750m you reach a crossroads. Turn east and follow this subsidiary track to Llyn y Gadair. Go around the lake to the base of the arête and then into the gully on its right-hand side. Seek out a large pinnacle in the bed of the gully with a leaning pinnacle above. Table Direct starts up a chimney above this.

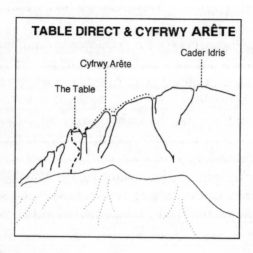

TABLE DIRECT & CYFRWY ARÊTE

Cader Idris

Cyfrwy Arête

The Table

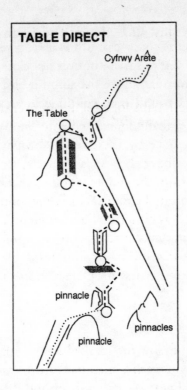

CLIMB

Pitch 1: Climb the chimney directly and then traverse right when you have cleared the top of it. Move steeply back left to a stance on a ledge. Belay here.

Pitch 2: Climb a corner (it has good holds) to a stance at the base of a rib. Belay here.

Pitch 3: Ascend the rib – which can be loose – and then cut left to follow a rising traverse left to the base of an arête.

Pitch 4: Climb the exposed arête directly to the top of the Table and belay there.

Pitch 5: You are now on the main crest of the arête. Scramble down into the gap between the Table and the main part of the ridge. A slanting crack provides an exit to a 'breche' (gap) and leads you on to the scrambling section.

Pitch 6: Superb, airy scrambling over short walls and ledges leads to the summit. Take care, however, as the rock can be loose.

DESCENT

A scree couloir to the south-east of the arête gives a direct descent to Llyn y Gadair. Cader Idris's summit lies close to hand and can be reached by traversing above the summit cliff for 500m to the east. A convenient round is to continue in an easterly direction and descend by the Foxes Path and then back to the Pony Path.

APPENDIX I

Emergency Procedures

This section is meant only as a guide and is in no way a substitute for proper first-aid training. It is a good idea to contact your local St John or St Andrew's Ambulance Brigade and arrange to go on one of their excellent courses.

FIRST AID
➤ Check breathing: if necessary, clear airways to remove obstructions.
➤ Recovery position: turn casualty on to their side and into the recovery position (unless spinal injury is suspected).
➤ Check for severe bleeding: elevate the limb and apply direct pressure to a bleeding wound.
➤ Check for broken bones: do not move if a spinal injury is suspected. Make improvised splints to immobilise other fractures.
➤ Monitor condition: keep casualty warm and comfortable and provide reassurance while waiting for the rescue services.

GETTING HELP
➤ Dial 999 and ask the operator for this specific mountain rescue service.
➤ Inform them of the number of casualties; the name of the casualty and the description of their injuries.
➤ Give them the precise location of casualty, including a six-figure grid reference (this should be double-checked by a second person at the accident location).
➤ If the casualty lies part of the way up a cliff/route, give the name of the cliff/route climbed so that the rescuers can decide whether to approach from the top or the bottom.

➤ Inform them of the time the accident happened and the nature of accident; and inform them of the prevailing weather conditions.

➤ Remain by the phone until a member of the mountain rescue team or a police officer arrives.

HELICOPTER DRILLS

➤ Remove hats and secure all loose equipment before the arrival of the helicopter.

➤ Identify yourselves by raising your arms in a V-shape as the helicopter approaches – do not wave.

➤ If possible, stand with your back to the wind.

➤ Protect the injured person from the rotor down-draught.

➤ Allow the winchman to land when ready.

➤ Do not attempt to touch the winch rope or harness until it has touched the ground and the static electricity has earthed.

➤ Do not approach the helicopter unless directed to do so by one of the crew. When you do approach, you must be fully aware of the danger areas formed by the main rotor blades, the rear rotor and the jet exhausts.

APPENDIX II

Useful Addresses

British Mountaineering Council
177-179 Burton Road, West Didsbury,
Manchester M20 2BB
Tel: 0161 445 4747 Fax: 0161 445 4500

Plas y Brenin
The National Mountain Centre,
Capel Curig,
Gwynedd LL24 0ET
Tel: 01690 720214

The Association of British Mountain Guides (ABMG)
The Secretary, Daneville House, William Street, Penrith,
Cumbria

Fell and Rock Climbing Club
7 Troon Close, Stockport,
Cheshire SK7 2LF

Climbers' Club
1 Tai Orwig Terrace, Bryn Refail, Caernarvon,
Gwynedd LL55 3NY

YHA National Office
8 St Stephen's Hill, St Albans,
Herts AL1 2DY
Tel: 01727 855215 Fax: 01727 844126

Commercial Mountaineering Instructors
(MIC qualified and members of the Association of Mountaineering Instructors)

Covering the Lake District:
John White
John White Mountaineering
Garden Cottage, High Close, Langdale, Ambleside,
Cumbria LA22 9HH
Tel: 01539 437387

Covering Snowdonia:
Ross Ashe-Creggan
AC Ventures
Namaste, Morfa Crescent, Tywyn,
Gwynedd LL36 9AY
Tel/fax: (01654) 711389
email: ross@ac-adventures.freeserve.co.uk

BIBLIOGRAPHY

Ashcroft, J.B., *Britain's Highest Peaks* (David & Charles)

Ashcroft, R.N., *Britain's Alpine Ridges* (Crowood)

Ashton, S., *100 Classic Climbs in the Lake District* (Crowood)

Ashton, S., *100 Classic Climbs in Snowdonia* (Crowood)

Climber's Club, *Regional Climbing Guides, Snowdonia* (Climber's Club)

Fell and Rock Climbing Club, *Regional Climbing Guides, Lake District* (Fell and Rock Climbing Club)

Fyffe, A. and Peters, I., *The Handbook of Climbing* (Pelham Books)

Unsworth, W., *Encyclopedia of Mountaineering* (Hodder & Stoughton)

Wilson, K., *Classic Rock* (Baton Wicks)